# COLOSSIANS & PHILEMON

*Completion and Reconciliation in Christ*

## JOHN MACARTHUR

THOMAS NELSON

*Since 1798*

COLOSSIANS AND PHILEMON
MACARTHUR BIBLE STUDIES

© 2007 by John MacArthur.

John MacArthur
"Unleashing God's Truth, One Verse at a Time®"
"Unleashing God's Truth, One Verse at a Time" is a trademark of Grace to You. All rights reserved.

Published in Nashville, Tennessee, by Nelson Books, an imprint of Thomas Nelson. Nelson Books and Thomas Nelson are registered trademarks of HarperCollins Christian Publishing, Inc.

Nelson Books titles may be purchased in bulk for education, business, fundraising, or sales promotional use. For information, please email SpecialMarkets@ThomasNelson.com

Produced with the assistance of the Livingstone Corporation. Project staff include Jake Barton, Mary Horner Collins, and Andy Culbertson. Project editor: Len Woods

Scripture quotations marked NKJV are taken from *The Holy Bible*, New King James Version®. © 1979, 1980, 1982, 1992 Thomas Nelson, Inc.

Scripture quotations marked NASB are taken from the New American Standard Bible®, © 1960, 1962, 1963, 1968, 1971, 1972, 1973, 1975, 1977, 1995 by The Lockman Foundation. Used by permission.

"Keys to the Text" and "Truth for Today" material is taken from the following sources:

*Colossians* (electronic ed.). MacArthur New Testament Commentary Series. © 1992, 1996 by John MacArthur. Published by Moody Press, Chicago, Illinois. Used by permission.

*The Freedom and Power of Forgiveness* (electronic ed.). © 1998 by John MacArthur. Published by Crossway Books: Wheaton, Illinois. Used by permission.

*The MacArthur Study Bible* (electronic ed.). John MacArthur, General Editor. © 1997 by Word Publishing. All rights reserved. Used by permission.

*Matthew* (electronic ed.). MacArthur New Testament Commentary Series. © 1989 by John MacArthur. Published by Moody Press, Chicago, Illinois. Used by permission.

*Nelson's New Illustrated Bible Dictionary*. R. F. Youngblood, F. F. Bruce, R. K. Harrison, eds. © 1995 by Thomas Nelson, Inc., Nashville, Tennessee.

*Philemon* (electronic ed.). MacArthur New Testament Commentary Series. © 1992, 1996 by John MacArthur. Published by Moody Press, Chicago, Illinois. Used by permission.

*Philippians*. MacArthur New Testament Commentary Series. © 2001 by John MacArthur. Published by Moody Press, Chicago, Illinois. Used by permission.

*What Does the Bible Say About . . . ?: The Ultimate A to Z Resource*. © 2001 by Thomas Nelson, Inc., Nashville, Tennessee.

Cover Art by Holly Sharp Design
Interior Design and Composition by Joel Bartlett, Livingstone Corporation

ISBN 978-0-7180-3512-9

*Printed in the United States of America.*

15 16 17 18 19 RRD 6 5 4 3 2 1

# CONTENTS

# INTRODUCTION TO COLOSSIANS

Colossians is named for the city of Colosse, where the church it was addressed to was located. It was also to be read in the neighboring church at Laodicea (4:16).

## AUTHOR AND DATE

Paul is identified as the author at the beginning of the letter. The testimony of the early church, including such key figures as Irenaeus, Clement of Alexandria, Tertullian, Origen, and Eusebius, confirms that the opening claim is genuine. Additional evidence for Paul's authorship comes from the book's close parallels with Philemon, which is universally accepted as having been written by Paul. Both were written (ca. AD 60–62) while Paul was a prisoner in Rome (4:3, 10, 18; Philem. 9–10, 13, 23); plus the names of the same people (Timothy, Aristarchus, Archippus, Mark, Epaphras, Luke, Onesimus, and Demas) appear in both epistles, showing that both were written by the same author at about the same time.

## BACKGROUND AND SETTING

Colosse was a city in Phrygia, in the Roman province of Asia (part of modern Turkey), about one hundred miles east of Ephesus, in the region of the seven churches of Revelation 1–3. The city lay alongside the Lycus River, not far from where it flowed into the Maender River. The Lycus Valley narrowed at Colosse to a width of about two miles, and Mt. Cadmus rose 8,000 feet above the city.

Colosse was a thriving city in the fifth century BC when the Persian king Xerxes (Ahasuerus, see Est. 1:1) marched through the region. Black wool and dyes (made from the nearby chalk deposits) were important products. In addition, the city was situated at the junction of the main north-south and east-west trade routes. By Paul's day, however, the main road had been rerouted through nearby Laodicea, thus bypassing Colosse and leading to its decline and the rise of the neighboring cities of Laodicea and Hierapolis.

Although Colosse's population was mainly Gentile, there was a large Jewish settlement dating from the days of Antiochus the Great (223–187 BC). Colosse's mixed population of Jews and Gentiles manifested itself both in the composition of the church and in the heresy that plagued it, which contained elements of both Jewish legalism and pagan mysticism.

The church at Colosse began during Paul's three-year ministry at Ephesus

(Acts 19). Its founder was not Paul, who had never been there (2:1), but Epaphras (1:5–7), who apparently was saved during a visit to Ephesus, then likely started the church in Colosse when he returned home. Several years after the Colossian church was founded, a dangerous heresy arose to threaten it—one not identified with any particular historical system. It contained elements of what later became known as Gnosticism. Gnosticism held that God is good, but matter is evil; that Jesus Christ was merely one of a series of emanations descending from God and being less than God (a belief that led them to deny His true humanity); and that a secret, higher knowledge above Scripture was necessary for enlightenment and salvation. The Colossian heresy also embraced aspects of Jewish legalism, e.g., the necessity of circumcision for salvation, observance of the ceremonial rituals of the Old Testament law (dietary laws, festivals, Sabbaths), and rigid asceticism. It also called for the worship of angels and mystical experience. Epaphras was so concerned about this heresy that he made the long journey from Colosse to Rome (4:12–13), where Paul was a prisoner.

This letter was written from prison in Rome (Acts 28:16–31) sometime between AD 60 and 62 and is, therefore, referred to as a Prison Epistle (along with Ephesians, Philippians, and Philemon). It may have been composed almost contemporaneously with Ephesians and initially sent with that epistle (Eph. 6:21–22; Col. 4:7–8). He wrote this letter to warn the Colossians against the heresy they faced. Paul sent the letter to them with Tychicus, who was accompanying the runaway slave Onesimus as he went back to his master, Philemon, a member of the Colossian church (4:7–9). Epaphras remained behind in Rome (see Philem. 23), perhaps to receive further instruction from Paul.

## HISTORICAL AND THEOLOGICAL THEMES

Colossians contains teaching on several key areas of theology, including the deity of Christ (1:15–20; 2:2–10), reconciliation (1:20–23), redemption (1:13–14; 2:13–14; 3:9–11), election (3:12), forgiveness (3:13), and the nature of the church (1:18, 24–25; 2:19; 3:11, 15). Also, as noted above, it refutes the heretical teaching that threatened the Colossian church (ch. 2).

## INTERPRETIVE CHALLENGES

Those cults that deny Christ's deity have seized upon the description of Him as "the firstborn over all creation" (1:15) as proof that He was a created being. Paul's statement that believers will be "holy, and blameless, and above reproach" if they "continue in the faith" (1:22–23) has led some to teach that believers can lose their salvation. Some have argued for the existence of purgatory based on Paul's statement, "I . . . fill up in my flesh what is lacking in the afflictions of Christ" (1:24), while others see support for baptismal regeneration (2:12). The identity of the epistle from Laodicea (4:16) has also prompted much discussion. These issues will be treated in the notes.

## NOTES

**1**

# THE GOSPEL TRUTH
*Colossians 1:1–8*

## DRAWING NEAR

Excluding the news about Jesus dying for our sins and offering us new life, what is the best news you've ever received?

_____

_____

_____

_____

If you were arrested and put on trial for being a Christian, what would be the strongest evidence that you are "guilty as charged"?

_____

_____

_____

_____

_____

## THE CONTEXT

As this epistle opened, Paul and Timothy greeted their fellow believers with thanksgiving. Rejoicing at the report of their faith brought to him by Epaphras (the founder of the church at Colosse), he characteristically expressed thanks that the Colossians heard the glorious gospel and that it bore fruit in their lives.

Following the salutation, Paul's words suggested seven aspects of the gospel: it is received by faith, results in love, rests in hope, reaches the world, reproduces fruit, is rooted in grace, and is reported by people. Before considering these aspects in more detail, take a brief look at the meaning of this key term that Paul uses.

## KEYS TO THE TEXT

*Gospel:* This term is from the Greek word *euangelion*, from which we derive the English word *evangelize*. It literally means "good news." It was often used in classical Greek to speak of the report of victory brought back from a battle. The gospel is the good news of Jesus' victory over Satan, sin, and death. It is also the good news that we, too, can triumph eternally over those enemies through Him. Scripture describes the gospel with several phrases. Acts 20:24 calls it "the gospel of the grace of God." Romans 1:9 designates it "the gospel of His Son," 1 Corinthians 9:12 as "the gospel of Christ," Ephesians 6:15 as "the gospel of peace," and Revelation 14:6 as the "eternal gospel." The gospel is also described as the "word of truth" (Col. 1:5) or the "message of truth" (Eph. 1:13). Those descriptions have given rise to our common expression "the gospel truth." People use that phrase when they want to stress their sincerity, so that what they say will be believed.

## UNLEASHING THE TEXT

Read Colossians 1:1–8, noting the key words and definitions next to the passage.

### Colossians 1:1–8 (NKJV)

1 *Paul, an apostle of Jesus Christ by the will of God, and Timothy our brother,*

2 *To the saints and faithful brethren in Christ who are in Colosse: Grace to you and peace from God our Father and the Lord Jesus Christ.*

3 *We give thanks to the God and Father of our Lord Jesus Christ, praying always for you,*

4 *since we heard of your faith in Christ Jesus and of your love for all the saints;*

5 *because of the hope which is laid up for you in heaven, of which you heard before in the word of the truth of the gospel,*

**Timothy** (v. 1)—Paul's co-laborer and true child in the faith was able to be with him because, although Paul was a prisoner, he had personal living quarters (Acts 28:16–31).

**saints** (v. 2)—those who have been separated from sin and set apart to God—the believers in Colosse

**faithful** (v. 2)—a word used in the New Testament exclusively for believers

**Colosse** (v. 2)—one of three cities in the Lycus River valley in the region of Phrygia, in the Roman province of Asia (part of modern Turkey), about one hundred miles east of Ephesus

**God and Father of our Lord Jesus Christ** (v. 3)—This designation was often used to show that Jesus was one in nature with God, as any true son is with his father. It was an affirmation of Christ's deity (see Rom. 15:6; 2 Cor. 1:3; 11:13; Eph. 1:3; 3:14; 1 Pet. 1:3).

**love for all the saints** (v. 4)—one of the visible fruits of true saving faith is love for fellow believers (John 13:34–35; Gal. 5:22; 1 John 2:10; 3:14–16).

**the hope which is laid up** (v. 5)—The believer's hope is inseparable from his faith.

6 *which has come to you, as it has also in all the world, and is bringing forth fruit, as it is also among you since the day you heard and knew the grace of God in truth;*

7 *as you also learned from Epaphras, our dear fellow servant, who is a faithful minister of Christ on your behalf,*

8 *who also declared to us your love in the Spirit.*

**in all the world** (v. 6)—The gospel was never intended for an exclusive group of people; it is good news for the whole world (Matt. 24:14; 28:19–20; Mark 16:15; Rom. 1:8, 14, 16; 1 Thess. 1:8). It transcends all ethnic, geographic, cultural, and political boundaries.

**fruit** (v. 6)—refers to the saving effect of gospel preaching and to the growth of the church

**Epaphras** (v. 7)—the likely founder of the church at Colosse

1) In this short passage, we gain a number of insights into the lives of the Colossian believers. What words and phrases did Paul use to describe this church and his relationship with it?

_____

_____

_____

_____

2) If this were the only passage in the Bible that described the gospel, what could you learn about God's good news, just from these eight verses?

_____

_____

_____

_____

_____

3) What hope did the Colossians have?

_____

_____

_____

_____

4) Paul mentioned "love" three times. What is the connection between the gospel and love?

_____

_____

_____

_____

_____

5) What do we learn about Epaphras?

_____

_____

_____

_____

_____

## GOING DEEPER

Right off the bat in his letter to the Colossians, Paul described the gospel in terms of how it radically changes people's lives. For more perspective on this great truth, read 1 John 4:7–16.

7   *Beloved, let us love one another, for love is of God; and everyone who loves is born of God and knows God.*

8   *He who does not love does not know God, for God is love.*

9   *In this the love of God was manifested toward us, that God has sent His only begotten Son into the world, that we might live through Him.*

10   *In this is love, not that we loved God, but that He loved us and sent His Son to be the propitiation for our sins.*

11   *Beloved, if God so loved us, we also ought to love one another.*

12   *No one has seen God at any time. If we love one another, God abides in us, and His love has been perfected in us.*

13   *By this we know that we abide in Him, and He in us, because He has given us of His Spirit.*

14   *And we have seen and testify that the Father has sent the Son as Savior of the world.*

15 *Whoever confesses that Jesus is the Son of God, God abides in him, and he in God.*

16 *And we have known and believed the love that God has for us. God is love, and he who abides in love abides in God, and God in him.*

## EXPLORING THE MEANING

6) What are some of the evidences the apostle John cites as "proof" that a person has truly been converted?

_____

_____

_____

_____

_____

7) How does John summarize the gospel (4:13–15)?

_____

_____

_____

_____

_____

8) Paul was so confident and upbeat, it's easy to forget that he wrote this epistle from prison. What can you learn from Paul's attitude in less-than-desirable circumstances?

_____

_____

_____

_____

9) Paul used the Greek word *pistis* for "faith," which means to be persuaded that something is true and to trust in it. But far more than mere intellectual assent, it also involves obedience. How does this definition of faith differ from the way many people think of faith?

_____

_____

_____

_____

_____

_____

## TRUTH FOR TODAY

Saving faith is carefully defined in Scripture and needs to be understood because there is a dead, nonsaving faith that provides false security (James 2:14–26). True saving faith contains repentance and obedience as its elements. Repentance is an initial element of saving faith, and it involves three elements: a turning to God, a turning from evil, and an intent to serve God. No change of mind can be called true repentance without all three. Repentance is not merely being ashamed or sorry over sin, although genuine repentance always involves an element of remorse. It is a redirection of the human will, a purposeful decision to forsake all unrighteousness and pursue goodness instead. The faith that saves involves more than mere intellectual assent and emotional conviction. It also includes the resolution of the will to obey God's commands and laws. Obedience is the hallmark of the true believer.

## REFLECTING ON THE TEXT

10) Why is obedience a mark of true faith?

_____

_____

_____

_____

_____

11) The Colossians learned or heard the gospel from Epaphras. Who taught it to you? With whom are you sharing the gospel?

_____

_____

_____

_____

_____

_____

_____

12) Paul said the gospel will bear fruit wherever it takes root. What are some of the most vivid evidences of life change that God's Spirit has produced in you since believing in Christ?

_____

_____

_____

_____

_____

_____

_____

## PERSONAL RESPONSE

Write out additional reflections, questions you may have, or a prayer.

_____

_____

_____

_____

## Additional Notes

# 2

# PAUL PRAYS FOR THE COLOSSIANS

*Colossians 1:9–14*

## DRAWING NEAR

Describe your current prayer habits. (For instance, do you have a set time, keep a prayer list, consciously spend time being still before God, intercede for others, and so on?)

_____

_____

_____

Do you have people in your life who pray for you regularly? What has that meant to you?

_____

_____

_____

## THE CONTEXT

The Bible is replete with examples of God's people praying for one another.

- Job prayed for his friends (Job 42:10).
- Moses prayed for Aaron and Miriam (Num. 12:13; Deut. 9:20).
- David prayed for Solomon (1 Chron. 29:18–19).
- Isaiah prayed for the people of God (Isa. 63:15–64:12).
- Jesus prayed for His disciples (John 17:9–24).
- The Jerusalem church prayed for Peter's release from prison (Acts 12:5).
- Epaphras prayed for the Colossians (Col. 4:12).

In the early church, the ministry of an apostle consisted primarily of teaching the Word and prayer (Acts 6:4). While Paul obviously gave rich instruction to the Colossians in his letter to them, he also shared some of his prayers for them. Specifically, it was Paul's constant prayer for the Colossians that they be filled with the knowledge of God's will. He knew that only when believers are controlled by that knowledge can they walk worthy of the Lord and please Him.

# Keys to the Text

*Knowledge:* In his prayer, Paul asked God to grant the Colossians knowledge, a term consisting of the normal Greek word for "knowledge" (*gnosis*) with an added preposition (*epi*), which intensifies the meaning. The knowledge Paul wanted the Colossians to have is a deep and thorough knowledge. Such knowledge is a central theme in Paul's writings. True biblical knowledge is not speculative but is shown in obedience. The Bible further warns of the danger of a lack of knowledge. Ephesians 4:13–14 tells us that lack of knowledge produces "children, tossed to and fro and carried about with every wind of doctrine" (NKJV).

# Unleashing the Text

Read Colossians 1:9–14, noting the key words and definitions next to the passage.

## Colossians 1:9–14 (NKJV)

**the knowledge of His will** (v. 9)—This is not an inner impression or feeling, but a deep and thorough knowledge of the will of God that is finally and completely revealed in the Word of God (3:16; Eph. 5:17; 1 Thess. 4:3; 5:18; 1 Tim. 2:4; 1 Pet. 2:13, 15; 4:19).

**wisdom and spiritual understanding** (v. 9)—"Spiritual" modifies both "wisdom" (the ability to accumulate and organize principles from Scripture) and "understanding" (the application of those principles to daily living).

9 *For this reason we also, since the day we heard it, do not cease to pray for you, and to ask that you may be filled with the knowledge of His will in all wisdom and spiritual understanding;*

10 *that you may walk worthy of the Lord, fully pleasing Him, being fruitful in every good work and increasing in the knowledge of God;*

11 *strengthened with all might, according to His glorious power, for all patience and longsuffering with joy;*

**walk worthy** (v. 10)—This is a key New Testament concept which calls the believer to live in a way that is consistent with his identification with the Lord who saved Him.

**being fruitful in every good work** (v. 10)—Spiritual fruit is the by-product of a righteous life. The Bible identifies spiritual fruit as leading people to Christ (1 Cor. 16:15), praising God (Heb. 13:15), giving money (Rom. 15:26–28), living a godly life (Heb. 12:11), and displaying holy attitudes (Gal. 5:22–23).

**increasing in the knowledge of God** (v. 10)—Spiritual growth cannot occur apart from this knowledge (1 Pet. 2:2; 2 Pet. 3:18).

**patience and longsuffering** (v. 11)—These terms are closely related and refer to the attitude one has during trials. "Patience" looks more at enduring difficult circumstances, while "longsuffering" looks at enduring difficult people.

12 *giving thanks to the Father who has qualified us to be partakers of the inheritance of the saints in the light.*

13 *He has delivered us from the power of darkness and conveyed us into the kingdom of the Son of His love,*

14 *in whom we have redemption through His blood, the forgiveness of sins.*

**qualified us** (v. 12)—The Greek word means "to make sufficient," "to empower," or "to authorize." God qualifies us only through the finished work of the Savior. Apart from God's grace through Jesus Christ, all people would be qualified only to receive His wrath.

**inheritance** (v. 12)—Literally, "for the portion of the lot." Each believer will receive his own individual portion of the total divine inheritance, an allusion to the partitioning of Israel's inheritance in Canaan (see Num. 26:52–56; 33:51–54; Josh. 14:1–2).

**in the light** (v. 12)—Scripture represents "light" intellectually as divine truth (Ps. 119:130) and morally as divine purity (Eph. 5:8–14; 1 John 1:5). The saints' inheritance exists in the spiritual realm of truth and purity where God Himself dwells (1 Tim. 6:16). Light, then, is a synonym for God's kingdom (see John 8:12; 2 Cor. 4:6; Rev. 21:23; 22:5).

**delivered us** (v. 13)—The Greek term means "to draw to oneself" or "to rescue" and refers to the believer's spiritual liberation by God from Satan's kingdom, which, in contrast to the realm of light with truth and purity, is the realm of darkness (see Luke 22:53) with only deception and wickedness (1 John 2:9, 11).

**kingdom** (v. 13)—In its basic sense, a group of people ruled by a king. More than just the future, earthly millennial kingdom, this everlasting kingdom (2 Pet. 1:11) speaks of the realm of salvation in which all believers live in current and eternal spiritual relationship with God under the care and authority of Jesus Christ.

**the Son of His love** (v. 13)—See Matthew 3:17; 12:18; 17:5; Mark 1:11; 9:7; Luke 3:22; 9:35; Ephesians 1:6; and 2 Peter 1:17. The Father gave this kingdom to the Son He loves, as an expression of eternal love. That means that every person the Father calls and justifies is a love gift from Him to the Son.

**redemption** (v. 14)—The Greek word means "to deliver by payment of a ransom" and was used of freeing slaves from bondage. Here it refers to Christ freeing believing sinners from slavery to sin (see 1 Cor. 1:30; Eph. 1:7).

**through His blood** (v. 14)—A reference not limited to the fluid, as if the blood had saving properties in its chemistry, but an expression pointing to the totality of Christ's atoning work as a sacrifice for sin. This is a frequently used metonym in the New Testament (see Eph. 1:7; 2:13; Heb. 9:14; 1 Pet. 1:19). The word *cross* (as in v. 20) is used similarly to refer to the whole atoning work (see 1 Cor. 1:18; Gal. 6:12, 14; Eph. 2:16).

**the forgiveness of sins** (v. 14)—The Greek word is a composite of two words that mean "to pardon" or "grant remission of a penalty."

1) What three things did Paul pray for the Colossians to be filled with (v. 9)?

_____

_____

_____

_____

_____

2) Identify the specific prayer requests Paul made in verses 10–11. Note the verbs used.

_____

_____

_____

_____

3) Why did Paul pray that the Colossians might have strength?

_____

_____

_____

_____

_____

4) What has God done for us through Christ?

_____

_____

_____

_____

_____

_____

## GOING DEEPER

The very first followers of Jesus noted His habits of prayer and said, "Lord, teach us to pray." Read Jesus' response in Luke 11:1–11.

1   *Now it came to pass, as He was praying in a certain place, when He ceased, that one of His disciples said to Him, "Lord, teach us to pray, as John also taught his disciples."*

2  So He said to them, "When you pray, say: Our Father in heaven, hallowed be Your name. Your kingdom come. Your will be done on earth as it is in heaven.

3  Give us day by day our daily bread.

4  And forgive us our sins, for we also forgive everyone who is indebted to us. And do not lead us into temptation, but deliver us from the evil one."

5  And He said to them, "Which of you shall have a friend, and go to him at midnight and say to him, 'Friend, lend me three loaves;

6  for a friend of mine has come to me on his journey, and I have nothing to set before him';

7  and he will answer from within and say, 'Do not trouble me; the door is now shut, and my children are with me in bed; I cannot rise and give to you'?

8  I say to you, though he will not rise and give to him because he is his friend, yet because of his persistence he will rise and give him as many as he needs.

9  "So I say to you, ask, and it will be given to you; seek, and you will find; knock, and it will be opened to you.

10  For everyone who asks receives, and he who seeks finds, and to him who knocks it will be opened.

11  If a son asks for bread from any father among you, will he give him a stone? Or if he asks for a fish, will he give him a serpent instead of a fish?"

## EXPLORING THE MEANING

5) What truths about prayer did Jesus disclose on this occasion with His disciples?

_____

_____

_____

_____

_____

_____

_____

_____

6) How does Christ's shed blood bring us redemption and forgiveness?

_____

_____

_____

_____

_____

_____

7) How are "light" and "darkness" contrasted in Paul's prayer (vv. 12–13)?

_____

_____

_____

_____

_____

8) In verse 11, Paul talks about the spiritual strength that comes to those who possess real knowledge of God's will. What are some specific ways God provides strength and power to His children?

_____

_____

_____

_____

_____

## TRUTH FOR TODAY

Giving thanks is too often demoted to a secondary place in the prayers of Christ's people. Our attitude in approaching God is often "Give me, give me." We are quick to make our requests and slow to thank God for His answers. Because God so often answers our prayers, we come to expect it. We forget that it is only by His grace that we receive anything from Him. The Bible repeatedly stresses the importance of giving thanks. "It is good to give thanks to the LORD, and to sing praises to Your name, O Most High" (Ps. 92:1 NKJV). "Whatever you do in word or deed, do all in the name of the Lord Jesus, giving thanks to God the Father through Him" (Col. 3:17 NKJV). "Let us continually offer the sacrifice of praise to God, that is, the fruit of our lips, giving thanks to His name" (Heb. 13:15 NKJV). Thanksgiving should permeate our speech, our songs, and our prayers.

## REFLECTING ON THE TEXT

9) Are you a thankful person? List three ways you can begin to cultivate a more grateful attitude today. (Start with this simple exercise: Jot down ten blessings in your life.)

_____

_____

_____

_____

_____

_____

_____

10) Through prayer, we can play a role in other people's spiritual growth. Who is on your regular "prayer list"? What ministers or missionaries, small group leaders or neighbors?

_____

_____

_____

_____

_____

_____

_____

11) Write out this prayer of Paul, and personalize it using your family's names. (For example: "Lord, I ask you to fill my son, John, with the knowledge of your will . . .")

_____

_____

_____

_____

_____

## PERSONAL RESPONSE

Write out additional reflections, questions you may have, or a prayer.

_____

_____

_____

_____

_____

_____

_____

_____

_____

_____

_____

_____

_____

_____

_____

# 3

# CHRIST'S PREEMINENCE

*Colossians 1:15–23*

## DRAWING NEAR

The Bible uses many titles and descriptions for Jesus Christ. All reveal something about His Person or work. Which of these names for Jesus mean the most to you? Why?

- Savior
- Lord/Master
- Rabbi/Teacher
- The Good Shepherd
- The Lamb of God
- Son of Man
- The Great Physician
- Creator
- Messiah
- Lion of the Tribe of Judah
- The Way, the Truth, and the Life
- Redeemer
- Other:

_____

_____

_____

_____

_____

_____

## THE CONTEXT

The Bible is supremely a book about the Lord Jesus Christ. The Old Testament records the preparation for His coming. The Gospels present Him as God in human flesh, who came into the world to save sinners. In Acts, the message of salvation in Christ begins to be spread throughout the world. But of all the teaching about Jesus Christ, no passage is more significant than Colossians 1:15–19. This dramatic and powerful passage removes any needless doubt or confusion over Jesus' true identity. It is vital to a proper understanding of the Christian faith.

Much of the heresy that threatened the Colossian church revolved around the Person of Christ. The heretics viewed Christ as one of many lesser spirit beings that emanated from God. They taught that spirit was good and matter was evil. Hence, the idea that God Himself would take on evil matter was absurd to them. They denied Jesus' humanity and deity. Paul meets these false ideas head-on and defends Christ's deity and His sufficiency to reconcile men to God.

## KEYS TO THE TEXT

*Image of the Invisible God:* The Greek word for "image" means "copy" or "likeness." From this term we get our English word *icon*, referring to a statue. Jesus Christ is the perfect image—the exact likeness—of God and is in the very form of God (John 1:14; Phil. 2:6), and has been so from all eternity. By describing Jesus in this manner, Paul emphasizes that He is fully God in every way.

*Reconcile:* The Greek word for "reconcile" (1:20) means "to change" or "exchange." Its New Testament usage refers to a change in the sinner's relationship to God. Man is reconciled to God when God restores man to a right relationship with Him through Jesus Christ. An intensified form for "reconcile" is used in this verse to refer to the total and complete reconciliation of believers and ultimately "all things" in the created universe. This text does not teach that, as a result, all will believe; rather, it teaches that all will ultimately submit (see Phil. 2:9–11).

## UNLEASHING THE TEXT

Read Colossians 1:15–23, noting the key words and definitions next to the passage.

## Colossians 1:15–23 (NKJV)

15 *He is the image of the invisible God, the firstborn over all creation.*

16 *For by Him all things were created that are in heaven and that are on earth, visible and invisible, whether thrones or dominions or principalities or powers. All things were created through Him and for Him.*

17 *And He is before all things, and in Him all things consist.*

18 *And He is the head of the body, the church, who is the beginning, the firstborn from the dead, that in all things He may have the preeminence.*

19 *For it pleased the Father that in Him all the fullness should dwell,*

20 *and by Him to reconcile all things to Himself, by Him, whether things on earth or things in heaven, having made peace through the blood of His cross.*

**The firstborn over all creation** (v. 15)—The Greek word for "firstborn" can refer to one who was born first chronologically, but most often refers to preeminence in position or rank. "Firstborn" in this context does not mean "first created" for several reasons: (1) Christ cannot be both "first begotten" and "only begotten" (see John 1:14, 18; 3:16); (2) if Paul was teaching that Christ was a created being, he was agreeing with the heresy he was writing to refute; and (3) it is impossible for Christ to be both created and the Creator of everything (v. 16). Thus Jesus is the firstborn in the sense that He has the preeminence and possesses the right of inheritance "over all creation." He existed before the creation and is exalted in rank above it.

**thrones or dominions or principalities or powers** (v. 16)—These are various categories of angels whom Christ created and over whom He rules. There is no comment regarding whether they are holy or fallen, since He is Lord of both groups. The purpose of His catalog of angelic ranks is to show the immeasurable superiority of Christ over any being the false teachers might suggest.

**All things were created through Him and for Him** (v. 16)—As God, Jesus created the material and spiritual universe for His pleasure and glory.

**He is before all things** (v. 17)—When the universe had its beginning, Christ already existed; thus, by definition, He must be eternal (Mic. 5:2; John 1:1–2; 8:58; 1 John 1:1; Rev. 22:13).

**consist** (v. 17)—Literally, "to hold together." Christ sustains the universe, maintaining the power and balance necessary for life's existence and continuity (see Heb. 1:3).

**head of the body** (v. 18)—Paul uses the human body as a metaphor for the church, of which Christ serves as the "head." Just as a body is controlled from the brain, so Christ controls every part of the church and gives it life and direction (see Eph. 4:15; 5:23).

**the beginning** (v. 18)—This refers to both source and preeminence. The church had its origins in the Lord Jesus (Eph. 1:4), and He gave life to the church through His sacrificial death and resurrection to become its sovereign Head.

**the firstborn from the dead** (v. 18)—Jesus was the first chronologically to be resurrected, never to die again. Of all who have been or ever will be raised from the dead, and that includes all men (John 5:28–29), Christ is supreme.

**all the fullness** (v. 19)—A term likely used by those in the Colossian heresy to refer to divine powers and attributes they believed were divided among various emanations. Paul countered that by asserting that the fullness of deity—all the divine powers and attributes—was not spread out among created beings, but completely dwelt in Christ alone (see 2:9).

**having made peace** (v. 20)—God and those He saved are no longer at enmity with each other.

**alienated . . . enemies** (v. 21)—The Greek term for "alienated" means "estranged," "cut off," or "separated." Before any were reconciled, all people were completely estranged from God (see Eph. 2:12–13). The Greek word for "enemies" can also be translated "hateful." Unbelievers hate God and resent His holy standard because they love their "wicked works" (see John 3:19–20; 15:18, 24–25). Actually, there is alienation from both sides, since God "hates all workers of iniquity" (Ps. 5:5).

21 *And you, who once were alienated and enemies in your mind by wicked works, yet now He has reconciled*

22 *in the body of His flesh through death, to present you holy, and blameless, and above reproach in His sight—*

23 *if indeed you continue in the faith, grounded and steadfast, and are not moved away from the hope of the gospel which you heard, which was preached to every creature under heaven, of which I, Paul, became a minister.*

**reconciled . . . through death** (vv. 21–22)—Christ's substitutionary death on the cross that paid the full penalty for the sin of all who believe made reconciliation possible and actual (see Rom. 3:25; 5:9–10; 8:3).

**holy . . . in His sight** (v. 22)—"Holy" refers to the believer's positional relationship to God—he is separated from sin and set apart to God by imputed righteousness. This is justification. As a result of the believer's union with Christ in His death and resurrection, God considers Christians as holy as His Son (Eph. 1:4; 2 Cor. 5:21).

**continue in the faith** (v. 23)—Those who have been reconciled will persevere in faith and obedience because, in addition to being declared righteous, they are actually made new creatures (2 Cor. 5:17) with a new disposition that loves God, hates sin, desires obedience, and is energized by the indwelling Holy Spirit (see John 8:30–32; 1 John 2:19).

**preached to every creature** (v. 23)—The gospel has no racial boundaries. Having reached Rome, where Paul was when he wrote Colossians, it had reached the center of the known world.


1) How did Paul argue convincingly for the deity of Jesus Christ (vv. 15–17)?

_____

_____

_____

_____

_____


2) What part did Jesus play in creation?

_____

_____

_____

_____

3) Twice Paul used the word *firstborn* to speak of Christ. What does this term suggest, and how does this concept compare with the phrase "that in all things He may have the preeminence"?

_____

_____

_____

_____

_____

_____

4) What is reconciliation? Define it simply.

_____

_____

_____

_____

_____

_____

5) What is *our* role in becoming the people God created us and saved us to be (v. 23)?

_____

_____

_____

_____

_____

_____

## GOING DEEPER

For more about the preeminence of Christ—His superior Person and work—read Hebrews 1.

1 *God, who at various times and in various ways spoke in time past to the fathers by the prophets,*

2 *has in these last days spoken to us by His Son, whom He has appointed heir of all things, through whom also He made the worlds;*

3 *who being the brightness of His glory and the express image of His person, and upholding all things by the word of His power, when He had by Himself purged our sins, sat down at the right hand of the Majesty on high,*

4 *having become so much better than the angels, as He has by inheritance obtained a more excellent name than they.*

5 *For to which of the angels did He ever say: "You are My Son, today I have begotten You"? And again: "I will be to Him a Father, and He shall be to Me a Son"?*

6 *But when He again brings the firstborn into the world, He says: "Let all the angels of God worship Him."*

7 *And of the angels He says: "Who makes His angels spirits and His ministers a flame of fire."*

8 *But to the Son He says: "Your throne, O God, is forever and ever; a scepter of righteousness is the scepter of Your kingdom.*

9 *You have loved righteousness and hated lawlessness; Therefore God, Your God, has anointed You with the oil of gladness more than Your companions."*

10 *And: "You, LORD, in the beginning laid the foundation of the earth, and the heavens are the work of Your hands.*

11 *They will perish, but You remain; and they will all grow old like a garment;*

12 *Like a cloak You will fold them up, and they will be changed. But You are the same, and Your years will not fail."*

13 *But to which of the angels has He ever said: "Sit at My right hand, till I make Your enemies Your footstool"?*

14 *Are they not all ministering spirits sent forth to minister for those who will inherit salvation?*

## Exploring the Meaning

6) What further insight about Jesus' identity do you gain from Hebrews 1?

_____

_____

_____

_____

_____

7) The word used in Hebrews 1:3 translated "express image" is the Greek term *charakte*, and refers to an engraving tool or stamp. The idea is that Jesus is the exact "stamp" or likeness of God. Why is it important to believe and defend that Jesus was God in the flesh, and not just a messenger sent from God?

_____

_____

_____

_____

_____

8) Not only did Jesus create the universe, but He also sustains it. He is the power behind every consistency in the universe. What are the implications of this truth to your faith right now?

_____

_____

_____

_____

_____

9) What is the connection between the fullness of Christ's deity (vv. 15–19) and the complete reconciliation of sinners (vv. 20–22)?

_____

_____

_____

_____

_____

## TRUTH FOR TODAY

One of the great tenets of Scripture is the claim that Jesus Christ is completely sufficient for all matters of life and godliness! He is sufficient for creation, salvation, sanctification, and glorification. He is so pure that there is no blemish, stain, spot of sin, defilement, lying, deception, corruption, error, or imperfection. He is so complete that there is no other God besides Him; He is the only begotten Son; all the treasures of wisdom and knowledge are in Him. He is the only Mediator between God and man; He is the Sun that enlightens, the Physician that heals, the Wall of Fire that defends, the Friend that comforts, the Pearl that enriches, the Ark that supports, and the Rock to sustain under the heaviest of pressures. He has no beginning and no end. He is the spotless Lamb of God. He is our Peace. He is our Hope. He is our Life. He is the Lion of Judah, the Living Word, the Rock of Salvation, the Eternal Spirit. He is the Ancient of Days, Creator and Comforter, Messiah. And He is the great I AM!

## REFLECTING ON THE TEXT

10) What new insight into the Person of Jesus Christ have you gained from this study? Is there something new you've learned that you did not understand before?

_____

_____

_____

_____

_____

11) How would your life look if you truly gave Christ the place of preeminence?

_____

_____

_____

_____

12) Think of the people in your sphere of influence who are still in desperate need of God's reconciling grace. List them below. How can you, like Paul, be a servant of the gospel (v. 23) this week, conveying God's invitation to reconciliation?

_____

_____

_____

_____

_____

_____

## PERSONAL RESPONSE

Write out additional reflections, questions you may have, or a prayer.

_____

_____

_____

_____

_____

_____

_____

_____

# ADDITIONAL NOTES

# 4

## PAUL'S VIEW OF MINISTRY
### Colossians 1:24–29

### DRAWING NEAR

What comes to mind when you hear the word "ministry"?

_____

_____

_____

_____

Make up a brief "ministry résumé," listing a few ministry activities in which you have participated (see example below). What were the most enjoyable ministry experiences for you? If you haven't been involved in any particular activities, what type of ministry would you like to try?

| Dates | Ministry | Task performed |
|---|---|---|
| _Example:_ _Summer 2004_ | _Youth group volunteer_ | _Taught a ninth grade boys' Sunday school class; chaperoned high school mission trip_ |
| | | |
| | | |
| | | |
| | | |
| | | |
| | | |
| | | |
| | | |

# The Context

Ministry is a topic that was dear to the heart of the apostle Paul, and it is a frequent theme in his letters. He never lost the sense of wonder that God would call him to the ministry, and he never tired of talking about it. Paul often spoke of his ministry when he needed to establish his authority and credibility. That was his aim in this passage. Colossians was written in part as a polemic against false teachers, and it was essential for Paul to defend his authority to speak for God. Otherwise, the false teachers would have dismissed what he wrote as merely his own opinion.

Having begun the epistle with a statement of his apostolic authority, Paul then gave a detailed look at the divine character of his ministry. He recited eight aspects of that ministry: the source of the ministry, the spirit of the ministry, the suffering of the ministry, the scope of the ministry, the subject of the ministry, the style of the ministry, the sum of the ministry, and the strength of the ministry.

# Keys to the Text

*Ministry:* This is a distinctive biblical idea that means "to serve" or "service." In the Old Testament the word *servant* was used primarily for court servants. During the period between the Old and New Testaments, it came to be used in connection with ministering to the poor (such as the work of the seven deacons in waiting on tables in Acts 6:1–7). Paul's practice was always to present the gospel to the Jews first in every city he visited, but his primary calling and ministry was to the Gentiles.

In reality, all believers are "ministers." The model, of course, is Jesus, who "did not come to be served, but to serve" (Mark 10:45 NKJV). Jesus equated service to God with service to others. Our unselfish service should especially be rendered through our spiritual gifts, which are given by God to the saints in order that they might minister to one another. (*Nelson's New Illustrated Bible Dictionary*)

*Mystery:* This refers to truth, hidden until now, but revealed for the first time to the saints in the New Testament. Such truth includes the mystery of the incarnate God (2:2–3, 9), Israel's unbelief (Rom. 11:25), lawlessness (2 Thess. 2:7), the unity of Jew and Gentile made one in the church (Eph. 3:3–6), and the rapture of the church (1 Cor. 15:51). Of all the mysteries God has revealed in the New Testament, the most profound is the one specifically identified in Colossians 1:27, "Christ in you, the hope of glory" (NKJV). The New Testament is clear that Christ, by the Holy Spirit, takes up permanent residence in all believers. The Old Testament predicted the coming of the Messiah, but it did not reveal that He would actually live in His redeemed church made up mostly of Gentiles. The New Testament reserved the honor of revealing the glory of this mystery. Believers, both Jew and Gentile, now possess the surpassing riches of the indwelling Christ.

## Unleashing the Text

Read Colossians 1:24–29, noting the key words and definitions next to the passage.

### Colossians 1:24–29 (NKJV)

24 *I now rejoice in my sufferings for you, and fill up in my flesh what is lacking in the afflictions of Christ, for the sake of His body, which is the church,*

25 *of which I became a minister according to the stewardship from God which was given to me for you, to fulfill the word of God,*

26 *the mystery which has been hidden from ages and from generations, but now has been revealed to His saints.*

27 *To them God willed to make known what are the riches of the glory of this mystery among the Gentiles: which is Christ in you, the hope of glory.*

28 *Him we preach, warning every man and teaching every man in all wisdom, that we may present every man perfect in Christ Jesus.*

29 *To this end I also labor, striving according to His working which works in me mightily.*

**my sufferings** (v. 24)—Paul's present imprisonment (Acts 28:16, 30)

**fill up . . . what is lacking** (v. 24)—Paul was experiencing the persecution intended for Christ. In spite of His death on the cross, Christ's enemies had not gotten their fill of inflicting injury on Him, so they turned their hatred on those who preached the gospel (see John 15:18, 24; 16:1–3). It was in that sense that Paul filled up what was lacking in Christ's afflictions.

**the sake of His body** (v. 24)—Paul's motivation for enduring suffering was to benefit and build Christ's church.

**stewardship** (v. 25)—A steward was a slave who managed his master's household, supervising the other servants, dispensing resources, and handling business and financial affairs. Since the church is God's household (1 Tim. 3:16), Paul assumed the task of caring for, feeding, and leading the churches, for which he was accountable to God.

**to fulfill the word of God** (v. 25)—This refers to Paul's single-minded devotion to completely fulfill the ministry God gave him, which was to preach the whole counsel of God to those to whom God sent him (Acts 20:27; 2 Tim. 4:7).

**Gentiles . . . Christ in you** (v. 27)—That believers, both Jew and Gentile, now possess the surpassing riches of the indwelling Christ is the glorious revealed mystery of which Paul writes (John 14:23; Rom. 8:9–10; Gal. 2:20; Eph. 1:7, 17–18; 3:8–10, 16–19).

**the hope of glory** (v. 27)—The indwelling Spirit of Christ is the guarantee to each believer of future glory (Rom. 8:11; Eph. 1:13–14; 1 Pet. 1:3–4).

**perfect** (v. 28)—To be complete or mature—to be like Christ. This spiritual maturity is defined in 2:2.

**I . . . labor, striving according to His working** (v. 29)—"Labor" refers to working to the point of exhaustion. The Greek word for "striving" gives us the English word "agonize" and refers to the effort required to compete in an athletic event.

1) How did Paul explain his suffering (v. 24)? What was its cause? Its purpose?

_____

_____

_____

_____

_____

2) What role did Paul insist that the Word of God play in ministry (see v. 25)?

_____

_____

_____

_____

_____

3) Typically, when Christians hear or use the word "stewardship" they think of giving money to the church. Is this what Paul meant in verse 25, or was his stewardship more than this?

_____

_____

_____

_____

_____

4) What was the mystery of which Paul spoke in this passage (see v. 27), and why is it so significant?

_____

_____

_____

_____

_____

5) List all the verbs Paul used in this passage to describe his ministry efforts. Spend a few minutes reflecting on his word choices. What conclusions can you draw about the proper exercise of ministry?

_____

_____

_____

_____

_____

## Going Deeper

Some modern ministers promote themselves and focus on prosperity and success. Compare this to Paul's perspective on ministry as found in 2 Corinthians 4.

1 *Therefore, since we have this ministry, as we have received mercy, we do not lose heart.*

2 *But we have renounced the hidden things of shame, not walking in craftiness nor handling the word of God deceitfully, but by manifestation of the truth commending ourselves to every man's conscience in the sight of God.*

3 *But even if our gospel is veiled, it is veiled to those who are perishing,*

4 *whose minds the god of this age has blinded, who do not believe, lest the light of the gospel of the glory of Christ, who is the image of God, should shine on them.*

5 *For we do not preach ourselves, but Christ Jesus the Lord, and ourselves your bondservants for Jesus' sake.*

6 *For it is the God who commanded light to shine out of darkness, who has shone in our hearts to give the light of the knowledge of the glory of God in the face of Jesus Christ.*

7 *But we have this treasure in earthen vessels, that the excellence of the power may be of God and not of us.*

8 *We are hard-pressed on every side, yet not crushed; we are perplexed, but not in despair;*

9 *persecuted, but not forsaken; struck down, but not destroyed—*

10 *always carrying about in the body the dying of the Lord Jesus, that the life of Jesus also may be manifested in our body.*

11 *For we who live are always delivered to death for Jesus' sake, that the life of Jesus also may be manifested in our mortal flesh.*

12 *So then death is working in us, but life in you.*

13 *And since we have the same spirit of faith, according to what is written, "I believed and therefore I spoke," we also believe and therefore speak,*

14 *knowing that He who raised up the Lord Jesus will also raise us up with Jesus, and will present us with you.*

15 *For all things are for your sakes, that grace, having spread through the many, may cause thanksgiving to abound to the glory of God.*

16 *Therefore we do not lose heart. Even though our outward man is perishing, yet the inward man is being renewed day by day.*

17 *For our light affliction, which is but for a moment, is working for us a far more exceeding and eternal weight of glory,*

18 *while we do not look at the things which are seen, but at the things which are not seen. For the things which are seen are temporary, but the things which are not seen are eternal.*

## EXPLORING THE MEANING

6) How does Paul's description in 2 Corinthians 4 enhance your understanding of some vital aspects of biblical ministry?

_____

_____

_____

_____

_____

_____

7) Paul's attitude of joy should be the spirit of ministry for every Christian. The sad reality is, however, that many Christians have lost the joy of serving the Lord. Given that the ministry is often difficult and demands hard work, how can Christians (whether clergy or laity) maintain an attitude of joy?

_____

_____

_____

_____

_____

_____

8) According to Paul, what should be the goal of all ministry (Col. 1:28)? How can we know when we've reached this goal?

_____

_____

_____

_____

_____

9) What are the everyday (and eternal) implications of this stunning truth?

_____

_____

_____

_____

_____

## Truth for Today

Because he was made a minister by sovereign call, Paul viewed his ministry as a stewardship from God. In Paul's day, *stewardship* meant to manage a household as a steward of someone else's possessions. The steward had oversight of the other servants and handled the business and financial affairs of the household. That freed the owner to travel and pursue other interests. Being a steward was thus a position of great trust and responsibility in the ancient world. The Bible speaks of the church as the household of God (1 Tim. 3:15), and all believers have the responsibility to manage the ministries the Lord has given them.

Joy is generated by humility. People lose their joy when they become self-centered, thinking they deserve better circumstances or treatment than they are getting. That was never a problem for Paul. Like all of God's great servants, he was conscious of his unworthiness. Facing the possibility of martyrdom, he wrote, "If I am being poured out as a drink offering on the sacrifice and service of your faith, I am glad and rejoice with you all" (Phil. 2:17 NKJV). Because he believed he deserved nothing, no circumstance could shake his joyous confidence that God was in control of his life.

## Reflecting on the Text

10) What keeps you from being a joyful steward of the gifts God has given you?

_____

_____

_____

_____

_____

_____

11) Paul endeavored to serve and honor God with all his might. At the same time, he knew the effective "striving," or work with eternal results, was being done by God through him (v. 29). When have you seen this principle most vividly at work in your own life?

_____

_____

_____

_____

_____

_____

12) Do you sense God's conviction to minister in some way more vigorously? In what ways? In what specific areas?

_____

_____

_____

_____

_____

13) Think of your own pastor (or the pastoral staff at your church). How can you express gratitude for their ministry in your life?

_____

_____

_____

_____

_____

_____

## Personal Response

Write out additional reflections, questions you may have, or a prayer.

_____

_____

_____

_____

_____

_____

_____

_____

_____

_____

_____

_____

_____

_____

_____

# ADDITIONAL NOTES

# 5

# CHRIST OVER PHILOSOPHIES

*Colossians 2:1–10*

## DRAWING NEAR

Identify several different religious or philosophical systems held by people you know.

_____

_____

_____

_____

With a million and one bogus ideas and competing "truth claims" circulating in the world, how can you avoid buying into a deceitful belief system?

_____

_____

_____

_____

## THE CONTEXT

From the dawn of recorded history, man has pondered the questions of ultimate reality: *Who am I? Why am I here? Where am I going?* Worldly philosophies ineptly try to answer those queries. The city of Colosse also had its philosophers. The church there faced the danger of being infiltrated by false teaching, as we do in our own day. The church has throughout its history fought to maintain its doctrinal purity. In this polemical section of Colossians, Paul attacked the false teachers head-on. The specific heresy threatening the Colossians is unknown. We can, however, reconstruct some of its tenets from 2:8–23, where Paul attacked the first element of the Colossian heresy: false philosophy. By way of a warning, he contrasts the deficiency of philosophy with the sufficiency of Christ.

Paul exhorted the Colossians to maintain their allegiance to both the deity and complete sufficiency of Jesus Christ. He reminded them that, in contrast to the claims of the false teachers, in Christ "are hidden all the treasures of wisdom

41

and knowledge" (Col. 2:3). That statement was a profound summation of the sufficiency of the Lord Jesus.

## Keys to the Text

*Philosophy:* The word *philosophy* is from the Greek word *philosophia*, literally, "love of wisdom." It appears only here in the New Testament. The word described any theory about God, the world, or the meaning of life. The first-century Jewish historian Josephus wrote, "There are three philosophical sects among the Jews. The followers of the first of whom are the Pharisees, of the second the Sadducees, and the third sect who pretends to be a severer discipline are called Essenes" (*Jewish Wars* 2.8.2). Thus, the term *philosophy* was broad enough to encompass religious sects. Most likely the false teachers in Colosse used it to refer to the transcendent, higher knowledge they supposedly had attained through mystical experience. Paul, however, equates the false teachers' philosophy with "empty deceit"—worthless deception.

## Unleashing the Text

Read Colossians 2:1–10, noting the key words and definitions next to the passage.

### Colossians 2:1–10 (NKJV)

**great conflict** (v. 1)—The word means "striving" and comes from the same root as in 1:29. Both the Colossians and Laodiceans were among those for whom Paul struggled so hard in order to bring them to maturity.

**Laodicea** (v. 1)—the chief city of Phrygia in the Roman province of Asia, located just south of Hierapolis in the Lycus River valley

1 For I want you to know what a great conflict I have for you and those in Laodicea, and for as many as have not seen my face in the flesh,

2 that their hearts may be encouraged, being knit together in love, and attaining to all riches of the full assurance of understanding, to the knowledge of the mystery of God, both of the Father and of Christ,

3 in whom are hidden all the treasures of wisdom and knowledge.

**full assurance of understanding** (v. 2)—"Understanding" of the fullness of the gospel, along with inner encouragement and shared love, mark mature believers who, thereby, enjoy the "assurance" of salvation.

**of God ... Christ** (v. 2)—See 4:3. Leaving out the phrase between "God" and "Christ," which was probably not in the original text, changes nothing. The point is that the mystery Paul refers to here is that the Messiah Christ is God incarnate Himself (see 1 Tim. 3:16).

**all the treasures** (v. 3)—See vv. 9–10; 1:19. The false teachers threatening the Colossians claimed to possess a secret wisdom and transcendent knowledge available only to the spiritual elite. In sharp contrast, Paul declared that all the richness of truth necessary for either salvation, sanctification, or glorification is found in Jesus Christ, who Himself is God revealed.

**4** *Now this I say lest anyone should deceive you with persuasive words.*

**5** *For though I am absent in the flesh, yet I am with you in spirit, rejoicing to see your good order and the steadfastness of your faith in Christ.*

**6** *As you therefore have received Christ Jesus the Lord, so walk in Him,*

**7** *rooted and built up in Him and established in the faith, as you have been taught, abounding in it with thanksgiving.*

**8** *Beware lest anyone cheat you through philosophy and empty deceit, according to the tradition of men, according to the basic principles of the world, and not according to Christ.*

**9** *For in Him dwells all the fullness of the Godhead bodily;*

**10** *and you are complete in Him, who is the head of all principality and power.*

**lest anyone should deceive you** (v. 4)—Paul did not want the Colossians to be deceived by the persuasive rhetoric of the false teachers, which assaulted the Person of Christ. That is why throughout chapters 1 and 2 he stressed Christ's deity and His sufficiency both to save believers and bring them to spiritual maturity.

**absent in the flesh . . . with you in spirit** (v. 5)—Because he was a prisoner, Paul was unable to be present with the Colossians. That did not mean, however, that his love and concern for them was any less (see 1 Cor. 5:3-4; 1 Thess. 2:17). Their "good order" and "steadfast faith" (both military terms depicting a solid rank of soldiers drawn up for battle) brought great joy to the apostle's heart.

**walk in Him** (v. 6)—"Walk" is the familiar New Testament term denoting the believer's daily conduct (1:10; 4:5). To walk in Christ is to live a life patterned after His.

**the faith** (v. 7)—The sense here is objective, referring to the truth of Christian doctrine. Spiritual maturity develops upward from the foundation of biblical truth as taught and recorded by the apostles.

**cheat you** (v. 8)—This is the term for robbery. It is referring to false teachers who are successful in getting people to believe lies and robbing them of truth, salvation, and blessings.

**the basic principles of the world** (v. 8)—Far from being advanced, profound knowledge, the false teachers' beliefs were simplistic and immature like all the rest of the speculations, ideologies, philosophies, and psychologies the fallen satanic and human system invents.

**fullness of the Godhead** (v. 9)—Christ possesses the fullness of the divine nature and attributes.

**bodily** (v. 9)—In Greek philosophical thought, matter was evil, and spirit was good. Thus, it was unthinkable that God would ever take on a human body. Paul refutes this false teaching by stressing the reality of Christ's incarnation. Jesus was not only fully God, but fully human as well.

**complete in Him** (v. 10)—See John 1:16 and Ephesians 1:3. Believers are complete in Christ by the imputed perfect righteousness of Christ and through the complete sufficiency of all heavenly resources needed for spiritual maturity.

**the head of all principality and power** (v. 10)—Jesus Christ is the creator and ruler of the universe and all its spiritual beings, not a lesser being emanating from God, as the Colossian errorists maintained.

1) In verses 1–5, Paul revealed a window into his motivations and hopes. What drove him? Why was he so willing to struggle in ministry to the Colossians?

_____

_____

_____

_____

_____

2) What words and phrases did Paul use to spell out the basics of the Christian's "walk" (vv. 6–7)?

_____

_____

_____

_____

_____

3) Summarize Paul's teaching about worldly philosophies (v. 8).

_____

_____

_____

_____

4) According to Paul, in what ways is Christ greater than all worldly philosophies?

_____

_____

_____

_____

5) What did Paul mean when he said that Christians are "complete" in Christ?

_____

_____

_____

_____

_____

_____

_____

## GOING DEEPER

One of the great concerns of the apostles was for believers to be grounded in the knowledge of Christ. Read 2 Peter 1:2–11.

2  *Grace and peace be multiplied to you in the knowledge of God and of Jesus our Lord,*

3  *as His divine power has given to us all things that pertain to life and godliness, through the knowledge of Him who called us by glory and virtue,*

4  *by which have been given to us exceedingly great and precious promises, that through these you may be partakers of the divine nature, having escaped the corruption that is in the world through lust.*

5  *But also for this very reason, giving all diligence, add to your faith virtue, to virtue knowledge,*

6  *to knowledge self-control, to self-control perseverance, to perseverance godliness,*

7  *to godliness brotherly kindness, and to brotherly kindness love.*

8  *For if these things are yours and abound, you will be neither barren nor unfruitful in the knowledge of our Lord Jesus Christ.*

9  *For he who lacks these things is shortsighted, even to blindness, and has forgotten that he was cleansed from his old sins.*

10  *Therefore, brethren, be even more diligent to make your call and election sure, for if you do these things you will never stumble;*

11  *for so an entrance will be supplied to you abundantly into the everlasting kingdom of our Lord and Savior Jesus Christ.*

## Exploring the Meaning

6) What truths did Peter want his readers to understand? What practical difference will such knowledge of Christ make in our lives?

_____

_____

_____

_____

_____

7) Paul used the image of being rooted in rich soil (Col. 2:6–7). That eternal planting took place at salvation when we received Christ. In what ways is Christ the source of our continued spiritual nourishment, growth, and fruitfulness?

_____

_____

_____

_____

_____

_____

8) How would obedience to the command of verses 6–7 give you the power to avoid the danger of verse 8?

_____

_____

_____

_____

_____

9) Nothing has changed in two thousand years. The purveyors of error still wrap their demonic teachings in fancy words. To abandon biblical truth for empty philosophy is like returning to kindergarten after earning a doctorate. How do you explain the fact that the world's philosophies see the claims of the Bible as being naive and simplistic, and worldly teaching as deep and sophisticated?

_____

_____

_____

_____

_____

_____

_____

_____

_____

## TRUTH FOR TODAY

As a result of the Fall, man is in a sad state of incompleteness. He is spiritually incomplete because He is totally out of fellowship with God. He is morally incomplete because he lives outside of God's will. He is mentally incomplete because he does not know ultimate truth. At salvation, believers are made complete. Believers are spiritually complete because they have fellowship with God. They are morally complete in that they recognize the authority of God's will. They are mentally complete because they know the truth about ultimate reality. To maintain, as the Colossian false teachers did, that those who were in Christ still lacked anything is absurd. Those who are "partakers of the divine nature" have, through God's divine power, been "all things that pertain to life and godliness" (2 Pet. 1:3 NKJV). All true believers are complete in Christ and do not need the teachings of any cult or false teacher.

Everyone has a choice, whether to follow human wisdom or to come to Christ. To follow human wisdom is to be kidnapped by the emissaries of Satan and his false system, which leaves a person spiritually incomplete. To come to Christ is to come to the One who alone offers completeness. May those of us who have found Christ never doubt His sufficiency by turning aside to follow any human wisdom.

## REFLECTING ON THE TEXT

10) What do you learn from this short passage regarding Paul's attitude and life about caring for others and serving them with all your heart?

_____

_____

_____

_____

_____

_____

11) When were you first "planted" into Christ? What things have helped you grow and sink your roots deeper into His love?

_____

_____

_____

_____

_____

_____

12) How would you be different if you put your full confidence in the biblical declaration that "you are complete in Christ"? Think through your day. What would change in the way you react to worldly philosophies, to people, and to setbacks in your life?

_____

_____

_____

_____

_____

## PERSONAL RESPONSE

Write out additional reflections, questions you may have, or a prayer.

# ADDITIONAL NOTES

# 6

# CHRIST OVER LEGALISM
### Colossians 2:11–23

## DRAWING NEAR

Paul strongly refuted legalism in the early church. How do you define the term "legalism"?

_____

_____

_____

_____

_____

What are some ways Christians today are tempted to "work" their way to heaven?

_____

_____

_____

_____

## THE CONTEXT

Today there is an onslaught of false teaching of unprecedented proportions. On every side the sufficiency of Jesus Christ is either openly or implicitly denied. False philosophy has infiltrated the church in the guise of psychology, which is all too often viewed as a necessary supplement to God's Word. Many lean toward mysticism, claiming to receive visions and extrabiblical revelations. Others are legalists, equating holiness with observing a list of cultural taboos. Still others urge the practice of asceticism, arguing that poverty or physical deprivation is the path to godliness. Pastors, elders, and other church leaders, who are responsible to warn the church against false teaching, are often the very ones proclaiming these errors.

The churches in the Lycus Valley also faced the danger of spiritual intimidation. False teachers were telling them that Jesus Christ was not sufficient, that they needed something more. These people believed they were privy to a higher level of spiritual knowledge and the secrets of spiritual illumination. This higher, hidden truth was beyond Jesus Christ and the Word. These heretics formed an elite, exclusive group that disdained "unenlightened" and "simplistic" Christians. They effectively beguiled some Christians and drew them away from confidence in Christ alone. The "something more" that the false teachers offered was a syncretism of pagan philosophy, Jewish legalism, mysticism, and asceticism. As noted earlier, Paul wrote the Colossians to refute that false teaching and to present the absolute sufficiency of Jesus Christ for salvation and sanctification. Because the Colossians had Christ, and He is sufficient, they did not need to be intimidated by the false teachers.

## Keys to the Text

*Circumcision:* Circumcision, removal of the male foreskin, was the physical sign of the Old Testament covenant God made with Abraham. God applied special religious significance to this act, identifying circumcised descendants as God's people. There was a health benefit, since disease could be kept in the folds of the foreskin, so removing it prevented this possibility. But the spiritual meaning was related to the need to cut away sin and be cleansed. It symbolized mankind's need for a cleansing of the heart. It was the outward sign of the cleansing of sin that comes by faith in God (Rom. 4:11; Phil. 3:3). At salvation, believers undergo a spiritual "circumcision" by putting off the body of the sins of the flesh (see Rom. 6:6). This is the new birth, the new creation in conversion.

*Baptism:* Christian baptism altered the significance of the ancient ritual, symbolizing the believer's identification with Christ in His death, burial, and resurrection. Baptism by water is the outward affirmation of the already accomplished inner transformation. In Christ, we died and were buried with Him, and we have also been united with Him in His resurrection. There is a new quality and character to our lives, a new principle of life. This speaks of the believer's regeneration. The old self has died with Christ, and the life we now enjoy is the new, divinely given life of Christ Himself.

## Unleashing the Text

Read Colossians 2:11–23, noting the key words and definitions next to the passage.

## Colossians 2:11–23 (NKJV)

11 *In Him you were also circumcised with the circumcision made without hands, by putting off the body of the sins of the flesh, by the circumcision of Christ,*

12 *buried with Him in baptism, in which you also were raised with Him through faith in the working of God, who raised Him from the dead.*

13 *And you, being dead in your trespasses and the uncircumcision of your flesh, He has made alive together with Him, having forgiven you all trespasses,*

14 *having wiped out the handwriting of requirements that was against us, which was contrary to us. And He has taken it out of the way, having nailed it to the cross.*

15 *Having disarmed principalities and powers, He made a public spectacle of them, triumphing over them in it.*

**dead in your trespasses** (v. 13)—So entrapped in the sphere of sin, the world (Eph. 2:12), the flesh (Rom. 8:8), and the devil (1 John 5:19) as to be unable to respond to spiritual stimuli; totally devoid of spiritual life. Paul further defines this condition of the unsaved in 1 Corinthians 2:14; Ephesians 4:17–19; and Titus 3:3.

**He has made alive together with Him** (v. 13)—Only through union with Jesus Christ (vv. 10–12) can those hopelessly dead in their sins receive eternal life (see Eph. 2:5). Note that God takes the initiative and exerts the life-giving power to awaken and unite sinners with His Son; the spiritually dead have no ability to make themselves alive (see Rom. 4:17; 2 Cor. 1:9).

**forgiven you all trespasses** (v. 13)—See 1:14. God's free (Rom. 3:24) and complete (Rom. 5:20; Eph. 1:7) forgiveness of guilty sinners who put their faith in Jesus Christ is the most important reality in Scripture.

**wiped out the handwriting** (v. 14)—Through Christ's sacrificial death on the cross, God has totally erased the unpayable debt we have incurred for violating His law (Gal. 3:10; James 2:10; see Matt. 18:23–27).

**nailed it to the cross** (v. 14)—This is another metaphor for forgiveness. The list of a crucified criminal's crimes were nailed to the cross with that criminal to declare the violations he was being punished for (as in the case of Jesus, as noted in Matt. 27:37). Believers' sins were all put to Christ's account, nailed to His cross as He paid the penalty in their place for them all, thus satisfying the just wrath of God against crimes requiring punishment in full.

**Having disarmed** (v. 15)—Revealing yet another element of the Cross's work, Paul tells that the Cross spelled the ultimate doom of Satan and his evil host of fallen angels (see Gen. 3:15; John 12:31; 16:11; Heb. 2:14).

**principalities and powers** (v. 15)—While His body was dead, His living, divine spirit actually went to the abode of demons and announced His triumph over sin, Satan, death, and hell.

**made a public spectacle . . . triumphing over them** (v. 15)—The picture is that of a victorious Roman general parading his defeated enemies through the streets of Rome. Christ won the victory over the demon forces on the cross, where their efforts to halt God's redemptive plan were ultimately defeated.

**food . . . drink** (v. 16)—Paul warns the Colossians against trading their freedom in Christ for a set of useless, man-made, legalistic rules. Legalism is powerless to save or to restrain sin. The false teachers sought to impose some sort of dietary regulations, probably based on the Mosaic law (see Lev. 11). Since they were under the New Covenant, the Colossians (like all Christians) were not obligated to observe the Old Testament dietary restrictions.

**festival** (v. 16)—the annual religious celebrations of the Jewish calendar (e.g., Passover, Pentecost, or Tabernacles; see Lev. 23)

**new moon** (v. 16)—the monthly sacrifice offered on the first day of each month (Num. 10:10; 28:11–14; Ps. 81:3)

**sabbaths** (v. 16)—The Old Testament Jewish celebration of the seventh day, which pictured God's rest from creation. The New Testament clearly teaches that Christ is the Lord of the Sabbath.

16 *So let no one judge you in food or in drink, or regarding a festival or a new moon or sabbaths,*

17 *which are a shadow of things to come, but the substance is of Christ.*

18 *Let no one cheat you of your reward, taking delight in false humility and worship of angels, intruding into those things which he has not seen, vainly puffed up by his fleshly mind,*

19 *and not holding fast to the Head, from whom all the body, nourished and knit together by joints and ligaments, grows with the increase that is from God.*

20 *Therefore, if you died with Christ from the basic principles of the world, why, as though living in the world, do you subject yourselves to regulations—*

21 *"Do not touch, do not taste, do not handle,"*

22 *which all concern things which perish with the using— according to the commandments and doctrines of men?*

23 *These things indeed have an appearance of wisdom in self-imposed religion, false humility, and neglect of the body, but are of no value against the indulgence of the flesh.*

**shadow . . . substance** (v. 17)—The ceremonial aspects of the Old Testament law (dietary regulations, festivals, sacrifices) were mere shadows pointing to Christ. Since Christ, the true reality, has come, the shadows have no value (see Heb. 8:5; 10:1).

**cheat you** (v. 18)—Paul warns the Colossians not to allow the false teachers to cheat them of their temporal blessings or eternal reward (see 2 John 8) by luring them into irrational mysticism.

**false humility** (v. 18)—Since the false teachers took great delight in it, their "humility" was actually pride, which God hates (Prov. 6:16–17).

**worship of angels** (v. 18)—the beginning of a heresy that was to plague the region around Colosse for several centuries and far beyond—a practice the Bible clearly prohibits (Matt. 4:10; Rev. 19:10; 22:8–9).

**which he has not seen** (v. 18)—Like virtually all cults and false religions, the teachings of the Colossian false teachers were based on visions and revelations they had supposedly received. Their claims were false, since Jesus Christ is God's final and complete revelation to mankind (Heb. 1:1–2).

**Fleshly mind** (v. 18)—This describes the unregenerate and is further defined in Ephesians 4:17–19.

**died with Christ** (v. 20)—refers to the believer's union with Christ in His death and resurrection by which he has been transformed to new life from all worldly folly

**basic principles** (v. 20)—These are the same as "the commandments and doctrines of men" (v. 22).

1) What does the "circumcision of Christ" mean? How are we circumcised in Christ?

_____

_____

_____

_____

_____

2) How do verses 12–15 demonstrate God's amazing grace and our complete forgiveness?

_____

_____

_____

_____

_____

3) Based on verses 16–19, what erroneous teachings were making the rounds in Colosse?

_____

_____

_____

_____

_____

4) Note the negative descriptions used by Paul in this passage. What were the consequences for those who let themselves be duped by these false teachers?

_____

_____

_____

_____

_____

_____

5) According to Paul, why is legalistic asceticism powerless to restrain sin or bring one to God?

_____

_____

_____

_____

_____

## GOING DEEPER

Over and over again, the New Testament writers hammer away at the truth that a vibrant walk with Christ always rests on a strong foundation of faith. Read Romans 6:1–8 for a powerful reminder of God's great salvation.

1   *What shall we say then? Shall we continue in sin that grace may abound?*
2   *Certainly not! How shall we who died to sin live any longer in it?*
3   *Or do you not know that as many of us as were baptized into Christ Jesus were baptized into His death?*
4   *Therefore we were buried with Him through baptism into death, that just as Christ was raised from the dead by the glory of the Father, even so we also should walk in newness of life.*
5   *For if we have been united together in the likeness of His death, certainly we also shall be in the likeness of His resurrection,*
6   *knowing this, that our old man was crucified with Him, that the body of sin might be done away with, that we should no longer be slaves of sin.*
7   *For he who has died has been freed from sin.*
8   *Now if we died with Christ, we believe that we shall also live with Him.*

## EXPLORING THE MEANING

6) How should the truth that we have died and been raised with Christ affect our everyday lives?

_____

_____

_____

_____

_____

7) The worship of angels was a heresy that plagued the Phrygian region (where Colosse was located) for centuries (v. 18). What was the appeal of this aberrant belief? Why are angels still so popular in our time and culture?

_____

_____

_____

_____

_____

8) What does it mean to "hold fast to the Head," which is Christ?

_____

_____

_____

_____

9) The Colossian errorists were attempting to gain righteousness through self-denial. While reasonable care and discipline of one's body *is* of temporal value (1 Tim. 4:8), it has no real eternal value. How can a believer find a healthy balance between helpful discipline and legalistic asceticism?

_____

_____

_____

_____

## TRUTH FOR TODAY

Legalism is the religion of human achievement. It argues that spirituality is based on Christ plus human works. It makes conformity to man-made rules the measure of spirituality. Legalism is useless because it cannot restrain the flesh. It is also dangerously deceptive, because inwardly rebellious and disobedient Christians, or even non-Christians, can conform to a set of external performance standards or rituals.

Believers, however, are complete in Christ, who has provided complete salvation, forgiveness, and victory. Therefore, Paul tells the Colossians not to sacrifice their freedom in Christ for a set of man-made rules. Paul's message to the Colossians is also a warning to us. We are not to be intimidated by false human philosophy, legalism, mysticism, or asceticism. We must hold fast to Christ, in whom we have been made complete.

## REFLECTING ON THE TEXT

10) How can you properly express your gratitude to God today for so great a salvation and forgiveness, as described in Colossians 2:11–15?

_____

_____

_____

_____

_____

_____

_____

_____

11) Of the assorted heresies making the rounds in ancient Colosse (all of which are still prevalent today), which ones do you find yourself most susceptible to? What have you learned here about defeating these enticing ideas?

_____

_____

_____

_____

_____

_____

_____

12) Think of someone you know who is caught up in error. Write that person's name down and pray diligently for God to give him or her the ability to discern truth from falsehood.

_____

_____

_____

_____

_____

_____

_____

_____

## Personal Response

Write out additional reflections, questions you may have, or a prayer.

_____

_____

_____

_____

_____

_____

_____

_____

_____

_____

_____

_____

# ADDITIONAL NOTES

# 7

# CHRISTIAN CONDUCT
*Colossians 3:1–17*

## DRAWING NEAR

Paul says we are to die to sin in our lives, and live for Christ. Yet in some Christian circles certain "minor" sins are tolerated. What unbiblical attitudes or actions are most often ignored by believers?

_____

_____

_____

_____

_____

Paul reminded the Colossians that they had been raised with Christ. We possess the eternal life of Christ and have been raised to live on another plane. How can this truth affect your daily life?

_____

_____

_____

_____

_____

## THE CONTEXT

As Paul turned to more practical things, he called his readers to be preoccupied with heavenly realities, which is the hallmark of true spirituality and the starting point of practical holiness. So it's surprising when Paul then talked about putting sin to death in our lives here and now. Didn't Paul say repeatedly that this had already been done? At the moment of salvation, the old self was crucified with Christ, and we were raised to new life, yes. But this positional reality must be worked out in the believer's practical living. There can be no holiness or maturity in a life where sin runs unchecked.

We have died to sin's penalty, but sin's power still can be strong. Paul listed some of the most common and troubling sins that believers face. That is why we must continually put sin to death by yielding to the Holy Spirit. Christians must dress themselves spiritually in accordance with their new identity. Negatively, they must "put off" the garment of the old, sinful lifestyle. Positively, they must "put on" the lifestyle of the new man.

## Keys to the Text

*Set Your Mind:* This can also be translated "think" or "have this inner disposition." As a compass points north, the believer's entire disposition should point itself toward the things of heaven. Heavenly thoughts can come only by understanding heavenly realities from Scripture.

*Old Man/New Man:* The "old man" is a believer's unregenerate self. The Greek word for "old" does not refer to something old in years but to something that is worn out and useless. The old self died with Christ, and the life we now enjoy is a new, divinely given life that is the life of Christ Himself (see Gal. 2:20). We have been removed from the unregenerate self's presence and control, so we should not follow its old sinful ways as if we were still under its evil influence. The "new man" is the regenerate self, which replaces the old man. This is the essence of what believers are in Christ. Although the old self is dead, sin retains a foothold in our temporal flesh with its corrupted desires.

## Unleashing the Text

Read Colossians 3:1–17, noting the key words and definitions next to the passage.

### Colossians 3:1–17 (NKJV)

**If** (v. 1)—better translated "since"

**you were raised** (v. 1)—This verb actually means "to be co-resurrected." Because of their union with Christ, at the moment of their conversion, believers spiritually go through the same death and resurrection that Christ experienced. They are now alive in Him and able to understand spiritual truths, realities, blessings, and the will of God. These glorious benedictions (see Eph. 1:3) are the privileges and riches of the heavenly kingdom, all of which are at our disposal. Paul called them "things above."

1 *If then you were raised with Christ, seek those things which are above, where Christ is, sitting at the right hand of God.*

2 *Set your mind on things above, not on things on the earth.*

**sitting at the right hand of God** (v. 1)—The position of honor and majesty (see Ps. 110:1; Luke 22:69; Acts 2:33; 5:31; 7:56; Eph. 1:20; Heb. 1:3; 8:1; 1 Pet. 3:22) that Christ enjoys as the exalted Son of God. That exaltation makes Him the fountain of blessing for His people (John 14:13–14; see 2 Cor. 1:20).

3 *For you died, and your life is hidden with Christ in God.*

4 *When Christ who is our life appears, then you also will appear with Him in glory.*

5 *Therefore put to death your members which are on the earth: fornication, uncleanness, passion, evil desire, and covetousness, which is idolatry.*

6 *Because of these things the wrath of God is coming upon the sons of disobedience,*

7 *in which you yourselves once walked when you lived in them.*

8 *But now you yourselves are to put off all these: anger, wrath, malice, blasphemy, filthy language out of your mouth.*

**you died** (v. 3)—The verb's tense indicates that a death occurred in the past. In this case at the death of Jesus Christ, where believers were united with Him, their penalty of sin was paid, and they arose with Him in new life.

**hidden with Christ in God** (v. 3)—This rich expression has a threefold meaning: (1) Believers have a common spiritual life with the Father and Son (1 Cor. 6:17; 2 Pet. 1:4); (2) the world cannot understand the full import of the believer's new life (Rom. 8:19; 1 Cor. 2:14; 1 John 3:2); and (3) believers are eternally secure, protected from all spiritual enemies, and have access to all God's blessings (John 10:28; Rom. 8:31–39; Heb. 7:25; 1 Pet. 1:4).

**When Christ . . . appears** (v. 4)—at His second coming (see Rev. 19:11–13, 15, 16)

**put to death** (v. 5)—This refers to a conscious effort to slay the remaining sin in our flesh (see Zech. 4:6; Eph. 5:18; 6:17; 1 John 2:14).

**fornication** (v. 5)—Also translated "immorality," it refers to any form of sexual sin (see 1 Thess. 4:3).

**uncleanness** (v. 5)—Also translated "impurity," this term goes beyond sexual sin to encompass evil thoughts and intentions as well (see Matt. 5:28; Mark 7:21–22; 1 Thess. 4:7).

**passion, evil desire** (v. 5)—Similar terms that refer to sexual lust. "Passion" is the physical side of that vice, and "evil desire" is the mental side (see James 1:15).

**covetousness** (v. 5)—Also rendered "greed" (literally, it means "to have more"). It is the insatiable desire to gain more, especially of things that are forbidden (see Ex. 20:17; Deut. 5:21; James 4:2).

**which is idolatry** (v. 5)—When people engage in either greed or the sexual sins Paul has cataloged, they follow their desires rather than God's, in essence worshiping themselves—which is idolatry (Num. 25:1–3; Eph. 5:3–5).

**wrath of God** (v. 6)—His constant, invariable reaction against sin

**sons of disobedience** (v. 6)—This expression designates unbelievers as bearing the very nature and character of the disobedient, rebellious sinfulness they love.

**in which you . . . once walked** (v. 7)—before their conversion (see Eph. 2:1–5; Titus 3:3–4)

**put off** (v. 8)—A Greek word used for taking off clothes (see Acts 7:58; Rom. 13:12–14; 1 Pet. 2:1). Like one who removes his dirty clothes at day's end, believers must discard the filthy garments of their old, sinful lives.

**anger** (v. 8)—a deep, smoldering bitterness; the settled heart attitude of an angry person (see Eph. 4:31; James 1:19–20)

**wrath** (v. 8)—Unlike God's settled and righteous wrath, this is a sudden outburst of sinful anger; usually the eruption that flows out of "anger" (see Luke 4:28; Acts 19:28; Eph. 4:31).

**malice** (v. 8)—From the Greek term that denotes general moral evil. Here it probably refers to the damage caused by evil speech (see 1 Pet. 2:1).

**blasphemy** (v. 8)—The normal translation of this word refers to God. But here, since it refers to people, it is better translated "slander." To slander people, however, is to blaspheme God (James 3:9; see Matt. 5:22; James 3:10).

**put off . . . put on** (v. 9–10)—
These words are the basis
for the command of verse 8.
Because the old man died in
Christ and the new man lives
in Christ—this is the essence of
new creation or regeneration (2
Cor. 5:17)—believers must put
off remaining sinful deeds and
must be continually renewed
into Christlikeness.

**old man** (v. 9)—the old, unregenerate self, originating in
Adam (see Eph. 4:22)

**renewed** (v. 10)—See Romans
12:2 and 2 Corinthians 3:18.

9 *Do not lie to one another, since you have put off the
old man with his deeds,*

10 *and have put on the new man who is renewed in
knowledge according to the image of Him who
created him,*

11 *where there is neither Greek nor Jew, circumcised
nor uncircumcised, barbarian, Scythian, slave nor
free, but Christ is all and in all.*

12 *Therefore, as the elect of God, holy and beloved, put
on tender mercies, kindness, humility, meekness,
longsuffering;*

This Greek verb contains a sense of contrast with the former reality. It describes a new quality of life
that never before existed (see Rom. 12:2; Eph. 4:22). Just like a baby is born complete but immature,
the new man is complete, but has the capacity to grow.

**knowledge** (v. 10)—a deep, thorough knowledge, without which there can be no spiritual growth or
renewal (2 Tim. 3:16–17; 1 Pet. 2:2)

**image of Him who created him** (v. 10)—It is God's plan that believers become progressively more like
Jesus Christ, the one who made them (see Rom. 8:29; 1 Cor. 15:49; 1 John 3:2).

**Greek** (v. 11)—a Gentile, or non-Jew

**Jew** (v. 11)—a descendant of Abraham through Isaac

**Scythian** (v. 11)—An ancient nomadic and warlike people that invaded the Fertile Crescent in the
seventh century BC. Noted for their savagery, they were the most hated and feared of all the so-called
barbarians.

**slave nor free** (v. 11)—A social barrier had always existed between slaves and freemen; Aristotle had
referred to the slave as "a living tool." But faith in Christ removed the separation (1 Cor. 12:13; Gal.
3:28; see Philem. 6).

**Christ is all and in all** (v. 11)—Because Jesus Christ is the Savior of all believers, He is equally the
all-sufficient Lord of them all.

**Therefore** (v. 12)—In view of what God has done through Jesus Christ for the believer, Paul described
the behavior and attitude God expects in response (vv. 12–17).

**elect of God** (v. 12)—This designates true Christians as those who have been chosen by God. No one
is converted solely by his own choice, but only in response to God's effectual, free, uninfluenced, and
sovereign grace (see Acts 13:46–48; Rom. 11:4–5).

**beloved** (v. 12)—Election means believers are the objects of God's incomprehensible special love (see
John 13:1; Eph. 1:4–5).

**tender mercies** (v. 12)—This may also be rendered "heart of compassion." It is a Hebraism that con-
notes the internal organs of the human body as used figuratively to describe the seat of the emotions
(see Matt. 9:36; Luke 6:36; James 5:11).

**kindness** (v. 12)—refers to a goodness toward others that pervades the entire person, mellowing all
harsh aspects (see Matt. 11:29–30; Luke 10:25–37)

**humility** (v. 12)—See Matthew 18:4; John 13:14–16; James 4:6, 10. This is the perfect antidote to the
self-love that poisons human relationships.

13 *bearing with one another, and forgiving one another, if anyone has a complaint against another; even as Christ forgave you, so you also must do.*

14 *But above all these things put on love, which is the bond of perfection.*

15 *And let the peace of God rule in your hearts, to which also you were called in one body; and be thankful.*

16 *Let the word of Christ dwell in you richly in all wisdom, teaching and admonishing one another in psalms and hymns and spiritual songs, singing with grace in your hearts to the Lord.*

17 *And whatever you do in word or deed, do all in the name of the Lord Jesus, giving thanks to God the Father through Him.*

**meekness** (v. 12)—Sometimes translated "gentleness," it is the willingness to suffer injury or insult rather than to inflict such hurts.

**longsuffering** (v. 12)—See also Romans 2:4. It is also translated "patience," the opposite of quick anger, resentment, or revenge, and thus epitomizes Jesus Christ (1 Tim. 1:16; see 2 Pet. 3:15). It endures injustice and troublesome circumstances with hope for coming relief.

**as Christ forgave you** (v. 13)—Because Christ as the model of forgiveness has forgiven all our sins totally (1:14; 2:13–14), believers must be willing to forgive others.

**bond of perfection** (v. 14)—A better rendering is "perfect bond of unity." Supernatural love poured into the hearts of believers is the adhesive of the church (see Rom. 5:5; 1 Thess. 4:9).

**the peace of God** (v. 15)—The Greek word for "peace" here refers both to the call of God to salvation and consequent peace with Him, and to the attitude of rest or security (Phil. 4:7) believers have because of that eternal peace.

**word of Christ** (v. 16)—This is the Holy Spirit–inspired Scripture, the word of revelation He brought into the world.

**dwell in you richly** (v. 16)—"Dwell" means "to live in" or "to be at home," and "richly" may be more fully rendered "abundantly or extravagantly rich." Scripture should permeate every aspect of the believer's life and control every thought, word, and deed (see Ps. 119:11; Matt. 13:9; Phil. 2:16; 2 Tim. 2:15). This concept is parallel to being filled with the Spirit in Ephesians 5:18, since the results of each are the same. In Ephesians 5:18, the power and motivation for all the effects is the filling of the Holy Spirit; here it is the word richly dwelling. Those two realities are really one. The Holy Spirit fills the life controlled by His Word. This emphasizes that the filling of the Spirit is not some ecstatic or emotional experience, but a steady controlling of the life by obedience to the truth of God's Word.

**do all in the name of the Lord Jesus** (v. 17)—This simply means to act consistently with who He is and what He wants.

1) The beginning of chapter 3 forms a kind of bridge between what Paul has discussed in the first two chapters and what he will discuss now. What do verses 1–4 teach us about Christ? About believers?

_____

_____

_____

_____

2) Write down the different commands found in verses 5–11. Compare and contrast the command "put to death" with the command "put off."

_____

_____

_____

_____

_____

3) What are the specific behaviors that are forbidden (vv. 5–11)?

_____

_____

_____

_____

4) What positive, God-honoring traits and practices are encouraged (vv. 12–17)?

_____

_____

_____

_____

_____

5) How would you summarize the meaning of verse 17?

_____

_____

_____

_____

## Going Deeper

Paul said our life is "hidden with Christ" (3:3). No passage explains that glorious truth more eloquently than Romans 8:31–39. Take a few moments to read and ponder that passage.

31 *What then shall we say to these things? If God is for us, who can be against us?*

32 *He who did not spare His own Son, but delivered Him up for us all, how shall He not with Him also freely give us all things?*

33 *Who shall bring a charge against God's elect? It is God who justifies.*

34 *Who is he who condemns? It is Christ who died, and furthermore is also risen, who is even at the right hand of God, who also makes intercession for us.*

35 *Who shall separate us from the love of Christ? Shall tribulation, or distress, or persecution, or famine, or nakedness, or peril, or sword?*

36 *As it is written: "For Your sake we are killed all day long; we are accounted as sheep for the slaughter."*

37 *Yet in all these things we are more than conquerors through Him who loved us.*

38 *For I am persuaded that neither death nor life, nor angels nor principalities nor powers, nor things present nor things to come,*

39 *nor height nor depth, nor any other created thing, shall be able to separate us from the love of God which is in Christ Jesus our Lord.*

## Exploring the Meaning

6) In what specific ways are you motivated by the biblical declaration that we are accepted, loved, and secure because of our identity and union with Christ?

_____

_____

_____

_____

_____

_____

7) How does knowing that we are beloved by God motivate us to the conduct described in verses 12–16?

_____

_____

_____

_____

_____

_____

8) Thinking about "the things above" hones in on the spiritual values that characterize Christ, such as tenderness, kindness, humility, meekness, patience, wisdom, forgiveness, strength, purity, and love. Why is focusing on the realities of heaven so important?

_____

_____

_____

_____

_____

9) What does this passage teach about the consequences of refusing to put sin to death in our lives?

_____

_____

_____

_____

_____

## TRUTH FOR TODAY

Preoccupation with the eternal realities that are ours in Christ is to be the pattern of the believer's life. Jesus put it this way: "Seek first the kingdom of God and His righteousness, and all these things shall be added to you" (Matt. 6:33 NKJV). Paul is not advocating a form of mysticism. Rather, he desires that the Colossians' preoccupation with heaven govern their earthly responses. To be preoccupied with heaven is to be preoccupied with the One who reigns there and with His purposes, plans, provisions, and power. It is also to view the things, people, and events of this world through His eyes and with an eternal perspective.

Obviously, the thoughts of heaven that are to fill the believer's mind must derive from Scripture. The Bible is the only reliable source of knowledge about the character of God and the values of heaven. In it we learn the praiseworthy things our minds should dwell on (see Phil. 4:8). Such heavenly values dominating the mind will produce godly behavior.

## REFLECTING ON THE TEXT

10) List four practical things you could begin doing today to "set your mind on things above."

_____

_____

_____

_____

_____

11) In Paul's list of sinful attitudes and actions, which ones do you need to "put off"? How does one do this?

_____

_____

_____

_____

_____

12) What would it look like in your life if you did everything "in the name of the Lord Jesus"? Give examples of:

⟋ *Parenting* in the name of the Lord Jesus:

⟋ *Shopping* in the name of the Lord Jesus:

⟋ *Talking on the phone* in the name of the Lord Jesus:

⟋ *Working* in the name of the Lord Jesus:

⟋ *Driving* in the name of the Lord Jesus:

⟋ *Eating* in the name of the Lord Jesus:

⟋ *Serving* in the name of the Lord Jesus:

_____

_____

_____

_____

_____

## PERSONAL RESPONSE

Write out additional reflections, questions you may have, or a prayer.

_____

_____

_____

_____

_____

_____

_____

_____

_____

_____

_____

# 8

# THE CHRISTIAN HOME

*Colossians 3:18–21*

## DRAWING NEAR

What five words best describe your home life growing up?

_____

_____

_____

_____

From the following list, pick the ten most essential ingredients for a happy home:

_____ Spending time together

_____ Compassion

_____ A central devotion to Christ

_____ Limits on TV/media

_____ Kindness

_____ A stable income

_____ A realistic schedule

_____ Conflict resolution skills

_____ Family devotions

_____ Regular family meetings

_____ Honesty

_____ An attitude of servanthood

_____ Family traditions

_____ Parents who love each other deeply

_____ Meals together

_____ Church involvement

_____ Strong spiritual leadership

_____ Listening to one another

_____ A stay-at-home mom

_____ Clearly defined roles

_____ Annual vacations together

_____ The willingness to forgive

_____ Good communication

_____ Unselfishness

_____ Fun/laughter together

_____ Other:

## THE CONTEXT

Christianity is not just personal; it is relational. The life of the "new man" is a life lived among other newly transformed people. The new man is to have an impact also on the society in which he lives. Nowhere should the social aspect of the new man be more evident than in the home—the single most important social institution in the world. Genuine Christianity consists of both doctrine and holy living. The New Testament reminds us in many places that an intellectual knowledge of our faith must be accompanied by a life that proves faith's reality. And such a life can be lived only by vital contact with God through Christ. It is difficult to see how Christianity can have any positive effect on society if it cannot transform its own homes. In this passage Paul provides brief, direct instructions on Christian living in the home. He discusses the two primary relationships in ancient homes: husbands and wives, and parents and children.

## KEYS TO THE TEXT

*Submit:* The Greek verb means "to subject oneself," which denotes willingly putting oneself under someone or something. The term is used in Luke 2:51 to refer to Jesus' subjection to His parents, and in Romans 8:7, where Paul employs the word to speak of being submissive to the commands of God's law. It is helpful to note several misconceptions about submission. First, submission does not imply inferiority. Galatians 3:28 clearly affirms that spiritually there is no difference between male and female. Jesus submitted to the Father during His life on earth, yet He was in no way inferior to Him. Second, submission is not absolute. Obedience in this passage is reserved for children and servants. There may be times when a wife must refuse to submit to her husband's desires (if they violate God's Word). Finally, the husband's authority is not to be exercised in an authoritative, overbearing manner. The wife's submission takes place in the context of a loving relationship. That wives submit to their husbands is "fitting in the Lord." The Greek form in this phrase expresses an obligation, a necessary duty. It is how He designed and commands the family to operate.

*Love:* Husbands are commanded to "love" (Greek *agapate*) their wives. The present tense of the imperative indicates continuous action. It could be translated as "keep on loving." In other words, the love that existed from the start of the marriage is to continue throughout the marriage; it must never give way to bitterness. The verb itself seems best understood in the New Testament to express a willing love, not the love of passion or emotion, but the love of choice—a covenant kind of love.

## UNLEASHING THE TEXT

Read Colossians 3:18–21, noting the key words and definitions next to the passage.

## Colossians 3:18–21 (NKJV)

18 *Wives, submit to your own husbands, as is fitting in the Lord.*

19 *Husbands, love your wives and do not be bitter toward them.*

20 *Children, obey your parents in all things, for this is well pleasing to the Lord.*

21 *Fathers, do not provoke your children, lest they become discouraged.*

**love** (v. 19)—This is a call for the highest form of love, which is rendered selflessly (see Gen. 24:67; Eph. 5:22–28; 1 Pet. 3:7).

**be bitter** (v. 19)—The form of this Greek verb is better translated "stop being bitter," or "do not have the habit of being bitter." Husbands must not be harsh or angrily resentful toward their wives.

**Children** (v. 20)—The Greek word is *tekna*, a general term for children, not limited to a specific age group. It refers to any child still living in the home and under parental guidance.

**obey** (v. 20)—The present tense of the imperative demands a continuous obedience.

**in all things** (v. 20)—The only limit on a child's obedience is when parents demand something contrary to God's Word. For example, by coming to Christ, some children are acting contrary to their parents' wishes, yet it is permissible because God's Word takes precedence over parental authority (see Luke 12:51–53; 14:26).

**Fathers** (v. 21)—The Greek noun *pateres* should be translated "parents" as it is in Hebrews 11:23.

**provoke** (v. 21)—Also translated "do not exasperate," this word has the connotation of not stirring up or irritating.

**discouraged** (v. 21)—The idea of this term is "to be without courage, or spirit." It has the sense of being listless, sullen, discouraged, or despairing. Parents can cause their children to lose heart by failing to discipline them lovingly and instruct them in the ways of the Lord with balance.

1) What was Paul's inspired directive to wives?

_____

_____

_____

2) What is the two-part job description of a husband (one positive command and one "negative")?

_____

_____

_____

_____

_____

3) What behavior is expected of children? Why?

_____

_____

_____

_____

4) What instruction is aimed at fathers in this passage?

_____

_____

_____

_____

5) What is the connection between these four straightforward verses and the deeper theological concepts of Colossians 1–2? For example, how could a failure to understand the preeminence of Christ (see 1:15–19) lead to problems in the home?

_____

_____

_____

_____

_____

## Going Deeper

For another similar description of the difference Christ makes in a person's relationships, read Ephesians 5:19–6:4.

19 *Speaking to one another in psalms and hymns and spiritual songs, singing and making melody in your heart to the Lord,*

20 *giving thanks always for all things to God the Father in the name of our Lord Jesus Christ,*

21 *submitting to one another in the fear of God.*

22 *Wives, submit to your own husbands, as to the Lord.*

23 *For the husband is head of the wife, as also Christ is head of the church; and He is the Savior of the body.*

24 *Therefore, just as the church is subject to Christ, so let the wives be to their own husbands in everything.*

25 *Husbands, love your wives, just as Christ also loved the church and gave Himself for her,*

26 *that He might sanctify and cleanse her with the washing of water by the word,*

27 *that He might present her to Himself a glorious church, not having spot or wrinkle or any such thing, but that she should be holy and without blemish.*

28 *So husbands ought to love their own wives as their own bodies; he who loves his wife loves himself.*

29 *For no one ever hated his own flesh, but nourishes and cherishes it, just as the Lord does the church.*

30 *For we are members of His body, of His flesh and of His bones.*

31 *"For this reason a man shall leave his father and mother and be joined to his wife, and the two shall become one flesh."*

32 *This is a great mystery, but I speak concerning Christ and the church.*

33 *Nevertheless let each one of you in particular so love his own wife as himself, and let the wife see that she respects her husband.*

6:1 *Children, obey your parents in the Lord, for this is right.*

2 *"Honor your father and mother," which is the first commandment with promise:*

3 *"that it may be well with you and you may live long on the earth."*

4 *And you, fathers, do not provoke your children to wrath, but bring them up in the training and admonition of the Lord.*

## Exploring the Meaning

6) What additional nuances, insights, or instructions for families are found in the Ephesians passage that are not included in the Colossians?

_____

_____

_____

_____

_____

_____

7) How does a husband's continuous, willing, sacrificial, and heroic love—when practiced faithfully—short-circuit modern feminists' objections to wives' submission?

_____

_____

_____

_____

_____

8) Children are to obey their parents "in all things." Are there ever times when it is appropriate for children to defy their parents? Explain.

_____

_____

_____

_____

9) How might the following common parental actions/habits cause children to become discouraged? (If you are a parent, measure yourself against these practices.)

- Overprotection, never allowing children any liberty, having strict rules about everything
- Showing favoritism
- Failing to show affection—both verbally and physically
- A lack of standards, too much freedom
- Excessive discipline, or discipline done in anger
- Excessive criticism
- Neglect or uninvolvement

_____

_____

_____

_____

_____

## Truth for Today

The two basic principles Paul mentions in this brief passage, authority and submission, are not unique to Christianity. It has always been God's plan for homes to operate on this basis. Christianity did, however, introduce several new elements to the home. First, Christianity introduced a new presence into the home, the Lord Jesus Christ. This new presence brings a new power. Christ is there, and His Spirit provides the power to make the family what it ought to be. Second, there is a new purpose: "Whatever you do in word or deed, do all in the name of the Lord Jesus" (Col. 3:17 NKJV). Finally, Christianity introduced a new pattern for the home: "Husbands, love your wives, just as Christ also loved the church" (Eph. 5:25 NKJV). The new pattern is Christ. He is the model for us to follow.

## Reflecting on the Text

10) What new insight have you gained about family relations from Paul's concise discussion?

_____

_____

_____

_____

_____

11) In what specific ways is God's Spirit nudging you with the truths of this passage? What needs to change in your marriage? In the way you relate to your parents? In the way you treat your children?

_____

_____

_____

_____

12) Pick one of these verses (whichever most applies to your role in the family) and memorize it. Reflect on it throughout this week.

# Personal Response

Write out additional reflections, questions you may have, or a prayer.

_____

_____

_____

_____

_____

_____

_____

_____

_____

_____

_____

_____

_____

_____

_____

_____

_____

_____

_____

_____

_____

_____

_____

# 9

## MASTERS AND SLAVES
*Colossians 3:22–4:1*

## DRAWING NEAR

What would be your dream job? Why?

_____

_____

_____

_____

_____

What do you like most about your work situation? What do you like least?

_____

_____

_____

_____

_____

_____

## THE CONTEXT

In addition to the relationships between spouses and between parents and children, ancient households across the Roman Empire also featured relationships between masters and slaves. (In our day, this relationship can largely be compared to that of employer and employee.) Under the direction of the Holy Spirit, Paul next addresses how faith in Christ should affect these interactions.

It should be noted upfront that although the Word of God never advocates slavery, New Testament literature accepts slavery as a social reality and seeks to instruct those in that system to behave in a godly manner. Certainly in the letter to Philemon (delivered at the same time as Colossians; see lesson 12 in this study guide), Paul upholds the duties of slave and master. Paul asked Philemon to treat his returned slave with kindness and forgiveness—restoring the relationship to its divine design. In short, the divinely inspired apostle upheld service to an earthly master as a way to serve the Lord.

79

## Keys to the Text

*Fearing God:* The word for "fear" (v. 22) is the Greek term *phoboumenoi*. It derives from the verb *phobeo* (from which we get our English word *phobia*) and has the basic meaning "to be afraid or alarmed" or, as in this context, "to be filled with deep reverence, respect, or awe." It expresses the feeling of a person who is in the presence of someone infinitely superior.

*Phobeo* is used to describe the reaction of the disciples when they saw Jesus walking on the water (Matt. 14:26) and to describe the reactions of the people after the raising of the widow's son at Nain (Luke 7:16) and after the healing of the demoniacs at Gerasa (Luke 8:37). It is used to describe Zacharias's response to the appearance of the angel (Luke 1:12) and the spectators' response when he regained his speech (v. 65). It is used of the shepherds when they heard the angels sing (Luke 2:9), of the guards at the garden tomb when the angels rolled the stone away (Matt. 28:2–4), and of the women after they visited the empty tomb (v. 8). It is used to describe the feelings of the people who witnessed the signs and wonders of Pentecost (Acts 2:43) and of men in the midst of the shattering events of the last days (Luke 21:26). It is used of the response of the people to the deaths of Ananias and Sapphira (Acts 5:5, 11) and to the demons overpowering the unbelieving sons of Sceva who tried to cast the demons out in Jesus' name (19:16–17).

## Unleashing the Text

Read Colossians 3:22–4:1, noting the key words and definitions next to the passage.

### Colossians 3:22–4:1 (NKJV)

**Bondservants** (v. 22)—slaves

**according to the flesh** (v. 22)—human inclination (see 2 Cor. 10:2–3)

**eyeservice** (v. 22)—Better translated "external service." It refers to working only when the master is watching, rather than recognizing that the Lord is always watching, and how our work concerns Him (vv. 23–24).

**reward of the inheritance** (v. 22)—The Lord ensures the believer that he will receive a just, eternal compensation for his efforts (see Rev. 20:12–13), even if his earthly boss or master does not compensate fairly (v. 25). God deals with obedience and disobedience impartially (see Acts 10:34; Gal. 6:7). Christians are not to presume upon their faith in order to justify disobedience to an authority or employer (see Philem. 18).

22 *Bondservants, obey in all things your masters according to the flesh, not with eyeservice, as men-pleasers, but in sincerity of heart, fearing God.*

23 *And whatever you do, do it heartily, as to the Lord and not to men,*

24 *knowing that from the Lord you will receive the reward of the inheritance; for you serve the Lord Christ.*

25 *But he who does wrong will be repaid for what he has done, and there is no partiality.*

4:1 *Masters, give your bondservants what is just and fair, knowing that you also have a Master in heaven.*

**Masters** (4:1)—There should be mutual honor and respect from Christian employers to their employees, based on their common allegiance to the Lord.

1) What specific *actions* should mark Christian "bondservants" or employees?

_____

_____

_____

_____

_____

_____

2) What *attitudes* should fill the hearts and minds of Christian workers?

_____

_____

_____

_____

_____

3) What did Paul suggest as the proper *motives* for diligence in the workplace?

_____

_____

_____

_____

_____

4) What behavior is expected of Christian "masters" or employers?

_____

_____

_____

_____

_____

_____

_____

5) What eternal realities should motivate employers?

_____

_____

_____

_____

_____

## GOING DEEPER

The apostle Paul gave "employer-employee" instructions to another church he planted—the church at Ephesus. Read his charge in Ephesians 6:5–9.

5   *Bondservants, be obedient to those who are your masters according to the flesh, with fear and trembling, in sincerity of heart, as to Christ;*

6   *not with eyeservice, as men-pleasers, but as bondservants of Christ, doing the will of God from the heart,*

7   *with goodwill doing service, as to the Lord, and not to men,*

8   *knowing that whatever good anyone does, he will receive the same from the Lord, whether he is a slave or free.*

9   *And you, masters, do the same things to them, giving up threatening, knowing that your own Master also is in heaven, and there is no partiality with Him.*

# EXPLORING THE MEANING

6) Compare these two very similar passages. In what ways are they alike? What details are found in Ephesians but not in the parallel section in Colossians? List the adverbs that describe the way or the manner in which employees are to work.

_____

_____

_____

_____

_____

7) Since work was a reality in Eden *before* the Fall (see Gen. 2:15), why do you think the word *work* has gained such a negative connotation?

_____

_____

_____

_____

8) What practical differences would mark the efforts of a worker who took seriously 3:23?

_____

_____

_____

9) What would be the positive consequences of a person who embraced and applied the biblical teachings in this passage? Might there be potentially *negative* consequences? If so, what?

_____

_____

_____

_____

## Truth for Today

Many of us will do our best as long as circumstances reward our efforts. But what happens if we work for a less-than-ideal boss, or if our company seems satisfied with mediocrity, or if we are treated unjustly? Are we as willing to pursue excellence when things aren't going our way? Joseph is an encouragement to anyone who lives and labors in a less-than-perfect world. Ending up in jail in a foreign land, Joseph maintained such a pursuit of excellence by applying himself to the task at hand rather than focusing on how he had been framed. As a slave he probably had no means of appeal anyway. So he turned the hardships of his life into opportunities for diligence and focus. God honored this attitude with achievements that would be considered amazing under any circumstances. Ultimately, Joseph the minority slave rose to power and status as the nation's second-in-command (Gen. 41:41–45).

So if you honor God in your work and pursue an attitude of excellence, will God reward you with power and prestige? There is no guarantee of that. However, Scripture does make a promise: "Whatever you do, do it heartily, as to the Lord and not to men, knowing that from the Lord you will receive the reward of the inheritance" (Col. 3:23–24 NKJV). God will reward you according to how you do your work. He challenges you to excellence! (*What Does the Bible Say About . . .?*)

## Reflecting on the Text

10) Perhaps at this point you are able to identify certain "nonexcellent" personal work attitudes or habits. What are they? (For example: making personal calls at work, arriving late, playing computer games, turning in sloppy work, treating customers with indifference, etc.)

_____

_____

_____

_____

_____

_____

_____

11) List three specific changes you intend to make in the way you work.

_____

_____

_____

_____

_____

12) If you are an employer, brainstorm a list of ten things you could do to honor or show appreciation to your employees.

_____

_____

_____

_____

_____

## PERSONAL RESPONSE

Write out additional reflections, questions you may have, or a prayer.

_____

_____

_____

_____

_____

_____

_____

_____

# ADDITIONAL NOTES

# 10

# THE SPEECH OF THE NEW MAN

*Colossians 4:2–6*

## DRAWING NEAR

Most children grow up hearing the rhyme "Sticks and stones may break my bones, but words will never hurt me." Were you taught this couplet as a child? What do you think of this idea that words are harmless?

In which of the following areas of speech do you struggle most (circle all that apply):

- Praising God
- Grumbling/complaining
- Arguing
- Cursing
- Yelling
- Telling people off
- Being critical
- Gossiping
- Other:

- Lying
- Flattering
- Sharing the gospel
- Speaking the truth in love
- Boasting/bragging
- Encouraging others/building them up
- Expressing gratitude

## THE CONTEXT

In an ancient story, it is said that Bios, a wise man of ancient Greece, was given an animal to sacrifice. He was instructed to send back to the donor the best and worst parts of the animal. Instead of receiving two body parts, the donor found that Bios had sent him only one—the tongue. The tongue is indeed the best and worst of man. Jesus said, "Out of the abundance of the heart the mouth speaks" (Matt. 12:34 NKJV). He was teaching an important spiritual principle: Speech reflects the kind of person you are. Because the tongue is so difficult to control, a person's speech becomes the truest indicator of his spiritual state (see Matt. 12:37).

In Colossians 4:2–6, Paul continues the discussion of the "new man" in Christ that he began in chapter 3. He has discussed the personal characteristics and the home life of the new man. In this passage he broadens the scope of his discussion and focuses on prayer, walking in wisdom, and the gracious speech of believers. Next to their thoughts, attitudes, and motives, the tongue is probably the most difficult area for believers to control. Paul emphasizes four areas: the speech of *prayer*, the speech of *proclamation*, the speech of *performance*, and the speech of *perfection*.

## KEYS TO THE TEXT

*Continue Earnestly:* The Greek word for "continue" means "to be courageously persistent" or "to hold fast and not let go." It refers here to perseverance in prayer. Paul is calling strongly on believers to persist in prayer. We are to continue "steadfastly in prayer," "praying always with all prayer and supplication," and to "pray without ceasing" (Rom. 12:12; Eph. 6:18; 1 Thess. 5:17 NKJV). Praying at all times is not necessarily limited to constant vocalizing of prayers to God. Rather, it refers to being conscious to consistently relate every experience in life to God. This does not, however, obviate the need for persistence and earnestness in prayer. Such persistence is illustrated repeatedly in Scripture. The 120 disciples gathered in the Upper Room were continually devoting themselves to prayer (Acts 1:14). The early church followed their example (see Acts 2:42).

## UNLEASHING THE TEXT

Read Colossians 4:2–6, noting the key words and definitions next to the passage.

## Colossians 4:2–6 (NKJV)

2 *Continue earnestly in prayer, being vigilant in it with thanksgiving;*

3 *meanwhile praying also for us, that God would open to us a door for the word, to speak the mystery of Christ, for which I am also in chains,*

4 *that I may make it manifest, as I ought to speak.*

5 *Walk in wisdom toward those who are outside, redeeming the time.*

6 *Let your speech always be with grace, seasoned with salt, that you may know how you ought to answer each one.*

**being vigilant** (v. 2)—In its most general sense this means to stay awake while praying. But Paul has in mind the broader implication of staying alert for specific needs about which to pray, rather than being vague and unfocused.

**a door** (v. 3)—an opportunity (1 Cor. 16:8–9; 2 Cor. 2:12)

**the mystery of Christ** (v. 3)—truth about Messiah, hidden until now, but revealed for the first time to the saints in the New Testament

**those . . . outside** (v. 5)—This refers to unbelievers. Believers are called to live in such a way that they establish the credibility of the Christian faith and that they make the most of every evangelistic opportunity.

**with grace** (v. 6)—to speak what is spiritual, wholesome, fitting, kind, sensitive, purposeful, complimentary, gentle, truthful, loving, and thoughtful

**seasoned with salt** (v. 6)—Just as salt not only flavors but prevents corruption, the Christian's speech should act not only as a blessing to others, but as a purifying influence within the decaying society of the world.

1) What specific instructions does Paul give about prayer in verses 2–4? What is the difference between praying and being devoted to prayer?

_____

_____

_____

_____

_____

2) What kind of speech did Paul regard as a duty (vv. 3–4)?

_____

_____

_____

_____

3) What verbal guidelines did Paul give for interacting with those who are "outside" (i.e. unbelievers)?

_____

_____

_____

_____

4) What does it mean to "redeem the time"?

_____

_____

_____

_____

_____

5) According to Paul, what are the standards for Christians when it comes to general conversation (v. 6)?

_____

_____

_____

_____

## GOING DEEPER

Our tongues can be used for glorious, God-honoring purposes, or they can be instruments of evil. Read James 3:2–12 for another window into these twin truths.

> 2 *For we all stumble in many things. If anyone does not stumble in word, he is a perfect man, able also to bridle the whole body.*
> 3 *Indeed, we put bits in horses' mouths that they may obey us, and we turn their whole body.*
> 4 *Look also at ships: although they are so large and are driven by fierce winds, they are turned by a very small rudder wherever the pilot desires.*
> 5 *Even so the tongue is a little member and boasts great things. See how great a forest a little fire kindles!*

6   *And the tongue is a fire, a world of iniquity. The tongue is so set among our members that it defiles the whole body, and sets on fire the course of nature; and it is set on fire by hell.*

7   *For every kind of beast and bird, of reptile and creature of the sea, is tamed and has been tamed by mankind.*

8   *But no man can tame the tongue. It is an unruly evil, full of deadly poison.*

9   *With it we bless our God and Father, and with it we curse men, who have been made in the similitude of God.*

10  *Out of the same mouth proceed blessing and cursing. My brethren, these things ought not to be so.*

11  *Does a spring send forth fresh water and bitter from the same opening?*

12  *Can a fig tree, my brethren, bear olives, or a grapevine bear figs? Thus no spring yields both salt water and fresh.*

## EXPLORING THE MEANING

6) How does reflecting on James 3 affect you? In other words, what verses in this passage do you find convicting? Encouraging?

_____

_____

_____

_____

7) In Colossians 4:3–4, Paul turns from a brief discussion of prayer (speech directed to God) to the proclamation of the gospel (speech directed to people). How does this passage lay a foundation for the common expression "Talk to God about men before you talk to men about God"?

_____

_____

_____

_____

_____

8) The idea behind verse 5 is that who believers *are* gives credibility to what they *say*. Everything we do (or don't do) speaks volumes about ourselves and our beliefs. How does a careless or sloppy lifestyle, or a life of legalism, diminish the power of our testimony to unbelievers?

_____

_____

_____

_____

_____

9) What does Paul mean when he urges believers to demonstrates speech "seasoned with salt"?

_____

_____

_____

_____

_____

_____

## TRUTH FOR TODAY

The Bible has much to say about the speech of both the redeemed and the unredeemed mouth. The unredeemed mouth is characterized by evil (Prov. 15:28), sexual immorality (Prov. 5:3), deceit (Jer. 9:8), curses (Ps. 10:7), oppression (Ps. 10:7), lies (Prov. 12:22), destruction (Prov. 11:11), vanity (2 Peter 2:18), flattery (Prov. 26:28), foolishness (Prov. 15:2), madness (Eccl. 10:12–13), carelessness (Matt. 12:36), boasting (Rom. 1:30), false doctrine (Titus 1:11), evil plots (Ps. 37:12), hatred (Ps. 109:3), too many words (Eccl. 10:14), and gossip (Prov. 26:22).

In contrast, redeemed speech is characterized by confession of sin (1 John 1:9), confession of Christ (Rom. 10:9–10), edifying speech (Eph. 4:29), talk of God's law (Ex. 13:9), praise to God (Heb. 13:15), blessing of enemies (1 Peter 3:9), talk about God (Ps. 66:16), wisdom and kindness (Prov. 31:26), and gentleness (Prov. 15:1). It takes as its model the Lord Jesus, who spoke instructively (Matt. 5:2), graciously (Luke 4:22), blamelessly (Luke 11:54), and without deceit (1 Peter 2:22).

## Reflecting on the Text

10) How often do you pray for opportunities to share the gospel (or for others to do so)?

_____

_____

_____

_____

_____

_____

11) In what specific ways is your speech "salty" (in the good sense)? How does your tongue serve as a purifying influence, rescuing conversations from the filth that so often marks public discourse?

_____

_____

_____

_____

_____

12) Look back over the items you circled in the list at the beginning of this lesson. With Paul's words in mind, what changes need to be made in your speech? Ask God to help you experience true life-change in the way you talk.

_____

_____

_____

_____

_____

## PERSONAL RESPONSE

Write out additional reflections, questions you may have, or a prayer.

# 11

## WITH A LITTLE HELP
## FROM MY FRIENDS
### *Colossians 4:7–18*

## DRAWING NEAR

Paul took time to honor and acknowledge the people who worked with him. What three people have been most encouraging and helpful in your own spiritual walk?

_____

_____

_____

_____

## THE CONTEXT

Leaders are much more effective if they have support and help. Proverbs 27:17 says, "As iron sharpens iron, so a man sharpens the countenance of his friend" (NKJV). Ecclesiastes 4:9 adds, "Two are better than one, because they have a good reward for their labor" (NKJV). Paul never ministered alone. He shared his first leadership opportunity in the church at Antioch with four other men, and throughout the following years of his missionary travels, he always had companions. The only time we find him alone in Acts is for a brief period in Athens (Acts 17). Although he was a prisoner as he wrote Colossians, he still was not alone. As he closed the letter, he included a kind of verbal group photograph. This parting passage features a number of Christians who helped him in his ministry while he was imprisoned at Rome.

The eight men named are not all well-known figures. Each was, however, a special person to Paul. And each was willing to pay the price of associating with a prisoner. That many of those mentioned had stuck with Paul for years indicates the tremendous loyalty he inspired. In this passage we meet the man with a servant's heart, the man with a sinful past, the man with a sympathetic heart, the man with a surprising future, the man with a strong commitment, the man with a single passion, the man with a specialized talent, and the man with a sad future. This section adds a warm, personal touch to what has been largely a doctrinal letter.

## Keys to the Text

*Tychicus:* The name means "fortuitous" or "fortunate." He was one of the Gentile converts Paul took to Jerusalem as a representative of the Gentile churches (Acts 20:4). A reliable companion of Paul and a capable leader, he was considered a replacement for Titus and Timothy on separate occasions (2 Tim. 4:12; Titus 3:12). Tychicus had been in Rome with Paul during his first imprisonment. He had the responsibility to deliver Paul's letters to the Colossians, to the Ephesians (Eph. 6:21), and to Philemon (Col. 4:9).

*Perfect:* The term is from the Greek word *teleios,* literally meaning "end," "limit," or "fulfillment." Paul used *teleios* to describe the completion or perfection of believers in Christ (1:28; 4:12). Christians move toward "perfection" and godliness when their faith matures through trials (James 1:4). Christians are made more complete by expressing God's love to others. Just as Paul pressed on toward the goal of perfection in his Christian walk (Phil. 3:12–14), so we, too, should make perfection in Christ our goal.

## Unleashing the Text

Read Colossians 4:7–18, noting the key words and definitions next to the passage.

### Colossians 4:7–18 (NKJV)

**Onesimus** (v. 9)—the runaway slave whose return to his master was the basis for Paul's letter to Philemon (see lesson 12)

**Aristarchus** (v. 10)—The Greek name of a Jewish native of Thessalonica (Acts 20:4; 27:2). He was one of Paul's companions who was seized by a rioting mob in Ephesus (Acts 19:29) and also accompanied Paul on his trip to Jerusalem and his voyage to Rome (Acts 27:4).

**Mark** (v. 10)—After having fallen out of favor with Paul for some time, Mark is seen here as one of Paul's key helpers (see 2 Tim. 4:11).

**Jesus who is called Justus** (v. 11)—possibly one of the Roman Jews who believed Paul's message (Acts 28:24)

7 *Tychicus, a beloved brother, faithful minister, and fellow servant in the Lord, will tell you all the news about me.*

8 *I am sending him to you for this very purpose, that he may know your circumstances and comfort your hearts,*

9 *with Onesimus, a faithful and beloved brother, who is one of you. They will make known to you all things which are happening here.*

10 *Aristarchus my fellow prisoner greets you, with Mark the cousin of Barnabas (about whom you received instructions: if he comes to you, welcome him),*

11 *and Jesus who is called Justus. These are my only fellow workers for the kingdom of God who are of the circumcision; they have proved to be a comfort to me.*

12 *Epaphras, who is one of you, a bondservant of Christ, greets you, always laboring fervently for you in prayers, that you may stand perfect and complete in all the will of God.*

13 *For I bear him witness that he has a great zeal for you, and those who are in Laodicea, and those in Hierapolis.*

14 *Luke the beloved physician and Demas greet you.*

15 *Greet the brethren who are in Laodicea, and Nymphas and the church that is in his house.*

16 *Now when this epistle is read among you, see that it is read also in the church of the Laodiceans, and that you likewise read the epistle from Laodicea.*

17 *And say to Archippus, "Take heed to the ministry which you have received in the Lord, that you may fulfill it."*

18 *This salutation by my own hand—Paul. Remember my chains. Grace be with you. Amen.*

**Epaphras** (v. 12)—The church at Colosse began during Paul's three-year ministry at Ephesus (Acts 19), when Epaphras apparently was saved during a visit to Ephesus. He likely started the church in Colosse when he returned home (see 1:5–7).

**Hierapolis** (v. 13)—a city in Phrygia twenty miles west of Colosse and six miles north of Laodicea

**Luke** (v. 14)—Paul's personal physician and close friend who traveled frequently with him on his missionary journeys and wrote the gospel of Luke and Acts

**Demas** (v. 14)—a man who demonstrated substantial commitment to the Lord's work before the attraction of the world led him to abandon Paul and the ministry (2 Tim. 4:9–10; Philem. 24)

**Nymphas and the church . . . in his house** (v. 15)—Other manuscripts make the name feminine (*Nympha*) and indicate the church met in her house, probably in Laodicea.

**when this epistle is read among you** (v. 16)—This letter was to be publicly read in the churches in Colosse and Laodicea.

**epistle from Laodicea** (v. 16)—A separate letter from Paul, usually identified as the epistle to the Ephesians. The oldest manuscripts of Ephesians do not contain the words "in Ephesus," indicating that in all likelihood it was a circular letter intended for several churches in the region. Tychicus may have delivered Ephesians to the church at Laodicea first.

**Archippus** (v. 17)—Most likely the son of Philemon (Philem. 2). Paul's message to him to fulfill his ministry is similar to the exhortation to Timothy (2 Tim. 4:5).

**by my own hand** (v. 18)—Paul usually dictated his letters to an amanuensis (recording secretary), but would often add his own greeting in his own writing at the end of his letters (see 1 Cor. 16:21; Gal. 6:11; 2 Thess. 3:17; Philem. 19).

**Remember my chains** (v. 18)—See Hebrews 13:3.

1) Looking only at verses 7 and 8, list everything you can about Tychicus. What were his spiritual credentials?

_____

_____

_____

2) Why was Paul's mention of Mark, the cousin of Barnabas, somewhat surprising? (Hint: see Acts 13:5, 13 and 15:36–41.)

_____

_____

_____

_____

3) What was Epaphras's special prayer for the believers?

_____

_____

_____

_____

4) Compare the mention of Demas (v. 14) with the statement in 2 Timothy 4:9–10. What became of Demas?

_____

_____

_____

5) What was Paul's message to Archippus?

_____

_____

_____

_____

## GOING DEEPER

For another glimpse of other friendships and ministry partners of Paul, read Romans 16:1–24.

1 *I commend to you Phoebe our sister, who is a servant of the church in Cenchrea,*
2 *that you may receive her in the Lord in a manner worthy of the saints, and assist her in whatever business she has need of you; for indeed she has been a helper of many and of myself also.*

3 *Greet Priscilla and Aquila, my fellow workers in Christ Jesus,*

4 *who risked their own necks for my life, to whom not only I give thanks, but also all the churches of the Gentiles.*

5 *Likewise greet the church that is in their house. Greet my beloved Epaenetus, who is the firstfruits of Achaia to Christ.*

6 *Greet Mary, who labored much for us.*

7 *Greet Andronicus and Junia, my countrymen and my fellow prisoners, who are of note among the apostles, who also were in Christ before me.*

8 *Greet Amplias, my beloved in the Lord.*

9 *Greet Urbanus, our fellow worker in Christ, and Stachys, my beloved.*

10 *Greet Apelles, approved in Christ. Greet those who are of the household of Aristobulus.*

11 *Greet Herodion, my countryman. Greet those who are of the household of Narcissus who are in the Lord.*

12 *Greet Tryphena and Tryphosa, who have labored in the Lord. Greet the beloved Persis, who labored much in the Lord.*

13 *Greet Rufus, chosen in the Lord, and his mother and mine.*

14 *Greet Asyncritus, Phlegon, Hermas, Patrobas, Hermes, and the brethren who are with them.*

15 *Greet Philologus and Julia, Nereus and his sister, and Olympas, and all the saints who are with them.*

16 *Greet one another with a holy kiss. The churches of Christ greet you.*

17 *Now I urge you, brethren, note those who cause divisions and offenses, contrary to the doctrine which you learned, and avoid them.*

18 *For those who are such do not serve our Lord Jesus Christ, but their own belly, and by smooth words and flattering speech deceive the hearts of the simple.*

19 *For your obedience has become known to all. Therefore I am glad on your behalf; but I want you to be wise in what is good, and simple concerning evil.*

20 *And the God of peace will crush Satan under your feet shortly. The grace of our Lord Jesus Christ be with you. Amen.*

21 *Timothy, my fellow worker, and Lucius, Jason, and Sosipater, my countrymen, greet you.*

22 *I, Tertius, who wrote this epistle, greet you in the Lord.*

23 *Gaius, my host and the host of the whole church, greets you. Erastus, the treasurer of the city, greets you, and Quartus, a brother.*

24 *The grace of our Lord Jesus Christ be with you all. Amen.*

## EXPLORING THE MEANING

6) What is your overall impression after reading Paul's personal greetings in Romans 16? What do you learn about Paul? About Christian fellowship?

_____

_____

_____

_____

_____

7) Why is it wiser to do ministry alongside others (rather than by yourself)?

_____

_____

_____

_____

_____

8) Paul mentioned how Aristarchus, Mark, and Justus "proved to be a comfort" to him. "Comfort" is the Greek word _paregoria_ and conveys the idea of supportive encouragement. Why is this such a crucial quality for those in ministry?

_____

_____

_____

_____

_____

9) How does Dr. Luke's service (Col. 4:14) show that not everyone in the Lord's service has to have a seminary degree?

_____

_____

_____

_____

## TRUTH FOR TODAY

Colossians presents a powerful case for the divinity of Jesus Christ. The theme of the book can be summed up in the words of Colossians 3:11: "Christ is all and in all." He is God (2:9); Creator (1:16); Savior (1:20; 2:13–14); and Head of the Church (1:18).

## REFLECTING ON THE TEXT

10) Epaphras fervently prayed for his fellow believers to be perfect and complete in God's will. For whom can you fervently pray this week?

_____

_____

_____

_____

11) It was Paul's desire for us to realize that "in all things [Christ] may have preeminence" (1:18). What steps can you take to put Christ first in your life?

_____

_____

_____

_____

12) What are the most vivid lessons you're taking away from this study of Colossians? How, by God's grace, do you intend to be different?

_____

_____

_____

_____

_____

## Personal Response

Write out additional reflections, questions you may have, or a prayer.

_____

_____

_____

_____

_____

_____

_____

_____

_____

_____

_____

_____

_____

_____

_____

_____

_____

_____

_____

_____

_____

_____

_____

_____

# Introduction to Philemon

Philemon, the recipient of this letter, was a prominent member of the church at Colosse (vv. 1–2; see Col. 4:9), which met in his house (v. 2). The letter was for him, his family, and the church.

## Author and Date

The book claims that the apostle Paul was its writer (vv. 1, 9, 19), a claim that few in the history of the church have disputed, especially since there is nothing in Philemon that a forger would have been motivated to write. It is one of the Prison Epistles, along with Ephesians, Philippians, and Colossians. Its close connection with Colossians, which Paul wrote at the same time (ca. AD 60–62; see vv. 1, 16), brought early and unquestioned vindication of Paul's authorship by the early church fathers (Jerome, Chrysostom, and Theodore of Mopsuestia). The earliest of New Testament canons, the Muratorian Canon (ca. AD 170), includes Philemon. Both Colossians and Philemon were written while Paul was a prisoner in Rome (Col. 4:3, 10, 18; Philem. 9–10, 13, 23).

## Background and Setting

Philemon had been saved under Paul's ministry, probably at Ephesus, several years earlier. Wealthy enough to have a large house (v. 2), Philemon also owned at least one slave, a man named Onesimus (literally, a common name for slaves). Onesimus was not a believer at the time he stole some money from Philemon and ran away (v. 18). Like countless thousands of other runaway slaves, Onesimus fled to Rome, seeking to lose himself in the Imperial capital's teeming and nondescript slave population. Through circumstances not recorded in Scripture, Onesimus met Paul in Rome and became a Christian.

The apostle quickly grew to love the runaway slave (vv. 12, 16) and longed to keep Onesimus in Rome (v. 13), where he was providing valuable service to Paul in his imprisonment (v. 11). But by stealing and running away from Philemon, Onesimus had both broken Roman law and defrauded his master. Paul knew those issues had to be dealt with and decided to send Onesimus back to Colosse. It was too hazardous for him to make the trip alone (because of the danger of slave-catchers), so Paul sent him back with Tychicus, who was returning to Colosse with the epistle to the Colossians (Col. 4:7–9). Along with Onesimus,

Paul sent Philemon this beautiful personal letter, urging him to forgive Onesimus and welcome him back to service as a brother in Christ (vv. 15–17).

## HISTORICAL AND THEOLOGICAL THEMES

Philemon provides valuable historical insights into the early church's relationship to the institution of slavery. Slavery was widespread in the Roman Empire (according to some estimates, slaves constituted one-third, perhaps more, of the population) and an accepted part of life. In Paul's day, slavery had virtually eclipsed free labor. Slaves could be doctors, musicians, teachers, artists, librarians, or accountants; in short, almost all jobs could be and were filled by slaves.

Slaves were not legally considered persons, but were the tools of their masters. As such, they could be bought, sold, inherited, exchanged, or seized to pay their master's debt. Their masters had virtually unlimited power to punish them, and sometimes did so severely for the slightest infractions. By the time of the New Testament, however, slavery was beginning to change. Realizing that contented slaves were more productive, masters tended to treat them more leniently. It was not uncommon for a master to teach a slave his own trade, and some masters and slaves became close friends. While still not recognizing them as persons under the law, the Roman Senate in AD 20 granted slaves accused of crimes the right to a trial. It also became more common for slaves to be granted (or to purchase) their freedom. Some slaves enjoyed very favorable and profitable service under their masters and were better off than many freemen because they were assured of care and provision. Many freemen struggled in poverty.

The New Testament nowhere directly attacks slavery; had it done so, the resulting slave insurrections would have been brutally suppressed and the message of the gospel hopelessly confused with that of social reform. Instead, Christianity undermined the evils of slavery by changing the hearts of slaves and masters. By stressing the spiritual equality of master and slave (v. 16; Gal. 3:28; Eph. 6:9; Col. 4:1; 1 Tim. 6:1, 2), the Bible did away with slavery's abuses. The rich theological theme that alone dominates the letter is forgiveness, a featured theme throughout New Testament Scripture (see Matt. 6:12–15; 18:21–35; Eph. 4:32; Col. 3:13). Paul's instruction here provides the biblical definition of forgiveness, without ever using the word.

# 12

# THE POWER OF FORGIVENESS
*Philemon 1–25*

## DRAWING NEAR

Which is harder: humbling yourself and seeking forgiveness from someone you've wronged, or letting go of bitterness and forgiving someone who has wronged you? Why?

_____

_____

_____

_____

## THE CONTEXT

Forgiveness is so important that God devoted an entire book of the Bible to it. Although it is the theme of the letter to Philemon, the word *forgiveness* does not appear in the book. Neither does the articulation of any doctrinal principles that would provide the theological foundation for forgiveness. Paul did not appeal to law or principle but to *love* (v. 9). He could do that because he knew Philemon to be a godly, spiritually mature man whose heart was right with God.

In the brief book of Philemon, the spiritual duty to forgive is emphasized, but not in principle, parable, or word picture. Through a real-life situation involving two people dear to him, Paul teaches the importance of forgiving others. Following the introduction in verses 1–3, Paul describes in verses 4–7 the spiritual character of one who forgives. Such a person has a concern for the Lord, a concern for people, a concern for fellowship, a concern for knowledge, a concern for glory, and a concern to be a blessing.

## KEYS TO THE TEXT

*Philemon:* This man was the slave owner whom Onesimus had wronged. He, too, had come to faith in Christ through Paul's ministry, possibly years before, during Paul's time in Ephesus (Acts 18–20; cf. 19:26). Philemon owned the home where the Colossian church met. He seems to have been a wealthy and influential man, at the opposite end of the social spectrum from Onesimus. Yet he was a devoted Christian, regarded by the apostle Paul as a beloved fellow worker.

*Sharing:* This word used in verse 6 is from the Greek word *koinonia*, often rendered "fellowship" or "communion." It has the root meaning of sharing something in common. This *koinonia* or "fellowship" means much more than simply enjoying one another's company. It refers to a mutual sharing of all life, which believers do because of their common life in Christ and mutual partnership in living out and spreading the gospel. It means we "belong to each other in the faith." Such fellowship was a great source of joy for Paul, as it is for all Christians who find strength, encouragement, support, comfort, and help through their communion with other believers.

## Unleashing the Text

Read Philemon 1–25, noting the key words and definitions next to the passage.

### Philemon 1–25 (NKJV)

**prisoner of Christ Jesus** (v. 1)—At the time of writing, Paul was a prisoner in Rome for the sake of and by the sovereign will of Christ. By beginning with his imprisonment and not his apostolic authority, Paul made this letter a gentle and singular appeal to a friend. A reminder of Paul's severe hardships was bound to influence Philemon's willingness to do the comparatively easy task Paul was about to request.

**Timothy** (v. 1)—He was not the coauthor of this letter, but prob-ably had met Philemon at Ephesus and was with Paul when the apostle wrote the letter. Paul mentions Timothy here and in the other epistles (2 Cor. 1:1; Phil. 1:1; Col. 1:1; 1 Thess. 1:1; 2 Thess. 1:1) because he wanted him recognized as a leader and the nonapostolic heir apparent to Paul.

1  *Paul, a prisoner of Christ Jesus, and Timothy our brother, to Philemon our beloved friend and fellow laborer,*

2  *to the beloved Apphia, Archippus our fellow soldier, and to the church in your house:*

3  *Grace to you and peace from God our Father and the Lord Jesus Christ.*

4  *I thank my God, making mention of you always in my prayers,*

5  *hearing of your love and faith which you have toward the Lord Jesus and toward all the saints,*

**Philemon** (v. 1)—A wealthy member of the Colossian church, which met in his house. Church buildings were unknown until the third century.

**Apphia, Archippus** (v. 2)—Philemon's wife and son, respectively

**in your house** (v. 2)—First-century churches met in homes, and Paul wanted this personal letter read in the church that met at Philemon's. This reading would hold Philemon accountable, as well as instruct the church on the matter of forgiveness.

**Grace to you** (v. 3)—The standard greeting that appears in all thirteen of Paul's New Testament letters. It highlighted salvation's means (grace) and its results (peace) and linked the Father and Son, thus affirming the deity of Christ.

6 *that the sharing of your faith may become effective by the acknowledgment of every good thing which is in you in Christ Jesus.*

7 *For we have great joy and consolation in your love, because the hearts of the saints have been refreshed by you, brother.*

8 *Therefore, though I might be very bold in Christ to command you what is fitting,*

9 *yet for love's sake I rather appeal to you—being such a one as Paul, the aged, and now also a prisoner of Jesus Christ—*

10 *I appeal to you for my son Onesimus, whom I have begotten while in my chains,*

11 *who once was unprofitable to you, but now is profitable to you and to me.*

12 *I am sending him back. You therefore receive him, that is, my own heart,*

13 *whom I wished to keep with me, that on your behalf he might minister to me in my chains for the gospel.*

14 *But without your consent I wanted to do nothing, that your good deed might not be by compulsion, as it were, but voluntary.*

15 *For perhaps he departed for a while for this purpose, that you might receive him forever,*

**effective** (v. 6)—Literally, "powerful." Paul wanted Philemon's actions to send a powerful message to the church about the importance of forgiveness.

**acknowledgment** (v. 6)—the deep, rich, full, experiential knowledge of the truth

**hearts** (v. 7)—This Greek word denotes the seat of human feelings (see the note on Col. 3:12, where the same Greek word is translated "tender mercies").

**refreshed** (v. 7)—This comes from the Greek military term that describes an army at rest from a march.

**bold . . . to command** (v. 8)—Because of his apostolic authority, Paul could have ordered Philemon to accept Onesimus.

**I rather appeal** (v. 9)—In this situation, however, Paul did not rely on his authority but called for a response based on the bond of love between himself and Philemon (v. 7; see 1 Cor. 10:1).

**the aged** (v. 9)—More than a reference to his chronological age (which at the time of this letter was about sixty), this description includes the toll that all the years of persecution, illnesses, imprisonments, difficult journeys, and constant concern for the churches had taken on Paul, making him feel and appear even older than he actually was.

**my son Onesimus** (v. 10)—To Paul, he was a son in the faith.

**begotten . . . in my chains** (v. 10)—While in prison at Rome, Paul had led him to faith in Christ.

**unprofitable . . . profitable** (v. 11)—Better translated "useless . . . useful," this is the same Greek root word from which "Onesimus" comes. Paul was making a play on words that basically said, "Useful formerly was useless, but now is useful." Paul's point was that Onesimus had been radically transformed by God's grace.

**voluntary** (v. 14)—Or, "of your own personal will." Paul wanted Onesimus to minister alongside him, but only if Philemon openly and gladly agreed to release him.

**perhaps** (v. 15)—Paul was suggesting that God providentially ordered the overturning of the evil of Onesimus's running away to produce eventual good (see Gen. 50:20; Rom. 8:28).

**more than a slave . . . beloved brother** (v. 16)—Paul did not call for Onesimus's freedom (see 1 Cor. 7:20–22), but asked that Philemon receive his slave now as a fellow-believer in Christ (see Eph. 6:9; Col. 4:1; 1 Tim. 6:2). Christianity never sought to abolish slavery, but rather to make the relationships within it just and kind.

**in the flesh** (v. 16)—in this physical life as they worked together

**in the Lord** (v. 16)—The master and slave were to enjoy spiritual oneness and fellowship as they worshiped and ministered together.

**with my own hand** (v. 19)—See 2 Thessalonians 3:17.

**even your own self** (v. 19)—Philemon owed Paul something far greater than the material debt Paul was offering to repay, since Paul had led him to saving faith, a debt Philemon could never repay.

**let me have joy** (v. 20)—By forgiving Onesimus, Philemon would keep the unity in the church at Colosse and bring joy to the chained apostle (see v. 7).

16 *no longer as a slave but more than a slave—a beloved brother, especially to me but how much more to you, both in the flesh and in the Lord.*

17 *If then you count me as a partner, receive him as you would me.*

18 *But if he has wronged you or owes anything, put that on my account.*

19 *I, Paul, am writing with my own hand. I will repay—not to mention to you that you owe me even your own self besides.*

20 *Yes, brother, let me have joy from you in the Lord; refresh my heart in the Lord.*

21 *Having confidence in your obedience, I write to you, knowing that you will do even more than I say.*

22 *But, meanwhile, also prepare a guest room for me, for I trust that through your prayers I shall be granted to you.*

23 *Epaphras, my fellow prisoner in Christ Jesus, greets you,*

24 *as do Mark, Aristarchus, Demas, Luke, my fellow laborers.*

25 *The grace of our Lord Jesus Christ be with your spirit. Amen.*

**even more than I say** (v. 21)—The "more than" forgiveness that Paul was urging upon Philemon was either: (1) to welcome Onesimus back enthusiastically, not grudgingly; (2) to permit Onesimus, in addition to his menial tasks, to minister spiritually with Philemon; or (3) to forgive any others who might have wronged Philemon. Whichever meaning Paul intended, he was not subtly urging Philemon to grant Onesimus freedom.

**a guest room** (v. 22)—literally, "a lodging," a place where Paul could stay when he visited Colosse

**I shall be granted to you** (v. 22)—Paul expected to be released from prison in the near future (see Phil. 2:23–24), after which he could be with Philemon and the other Colossians again.

**Mark, Aristarchus** (v. 24)—The story of the once-severed but now-mended relationship between Paul and Mark (Acts 15:38–40; 2 Tim. 4:11) would have been well-known to the believers in Colosse (Col. 4:10). Listing Mark's name here would serve to remind Philemon that Paul himself had worked through the issues of forgiveness, and that the instructions he was passing on to his friend were ones the apostle himself had already implemented in his relationship with John Mark.

1) What information about the man Philemon can you glean from this short letter? List the facts about him that are revealed here.

_____

_____

_____

_____

2) Paul revealed much about his personal situation and his history with Philemon (vv. 1–9). What key information do you see here that will prove to be leverage for what Paul was planning to ask Onesimus to do?

_____

_____

_____

_____

3) What words and phrases did Paul use to describe the changes in the runaway slave's life?

_____

_____

_____

_____

4) What are some of Paul's arguments for why Philemon should forgive Onesimus?

_____

_____

_____

_____

5) Do you think Paul's words in verses 17–21 are "manipulative"? Why or why not?

_____

_____

_____

_____

_____

_____

## GOING DEEPER

The gospel of Jesus Christ not only requires that we receive God's forgiveness; it also mandates that we offer forgiveness to those who have wronged us. Read the parable Jesus told in Matthew 18:21–35.

21 *Then Peter came to Him and said, "Lord, how often shall my brother sin against me, and I forgive him? Up to seven times?"*

22 *Jesus said to him, "I do not say to you, up to seven times, but up to seventy times seven.*

23 *Therefore the kingdom of heaven is like a certain king who wanted to settle accounts with his servants.*

24 *And when he had begun to settle accounts, one was brought to him who owed him ten thousand talents.*

25 *But as he was not able to pay, his master commanded that he be sold, with his wife and children and all that he had, and that payment be made.*

26 *The servant therefore fell down before him, saying, 'Master, have patience with me, and I will pay you all.'*

27 *Then the master of that servant was moved with compassion, released him, and forgave him the debt.*

28 *"But that servant went out and found one of his fellow servants who owed him a hundred denarii; and he laid hands on him and took him by the throat, saying, 'Pay me what you owe!'*

29 *So his fellow servant fell down at his feet and begged him, saying, 'Have patience with me, and I will pay you all.'*

30 *And he would not, but went and threw him into prison till he should pay the debt.*

31 *So when his fellow servants saw what had been done, they were very grieved, and came and told their master all that had been done.*

32 *Then his master, after he had called him, said to him, 'You wicked servant! I forgave you all that debt because you begged me.*

33 *Should you not also have had compassion on your fellow servant, just as I had pity on you?'*

34 *And his master was angry, and delivered him to the torturers until he should pay all that was due to him.*

35 *"So My heavenly Father also will do to you if each of you, from his heart, does not forgive his brother his trespasses."*

## EXPLORING THE MEANING

6) Summarize the central message of Christ's parable. Why should we forgive?

_____

_____

_____

_____

_____

_____

_____

_____

7) How did Paul handle the issue of slavery in writing to Philemon? Why didn't he condemn the practice altogether?

_____

_____

_____

_____

_____

_____

_____

8) How does Onesimus's experience reveal the power of the gospel? How does his changed life give you hope?

_____

_____

_____

_____

_____

9) Paul freely offered to accept Onesimus's penalty in order to renew the relationship between Onesimus and Philemon. In what ways is this a beautiful illustration of Christ's mediation for us?

_____

_____

_____

_____

_____

_____

_____

_____

_____

## TRUTH FOR TODAY

Vengeance is popular today; forgiveness is not. Retaliation is often portrayed as a virtue reflecting healthy self-esteem. It is heralded as an inalienable right of personal freedom. Vengeance is evidence of macho strength. Our sinful pride inclines us to respond this way. Pride always wants to demand eye-for-an-eye justice. We want to prolong punishment as long as possible and extract every ounce of suffering in return.

Forgiveness is not like that. It buries the offense as quickly as possible, even at the cost of personal pride. Paul was a very hard man to offend, simply because he would not take offense. That is a wonderful virtue. It is true godliness and genuine love in action: "[Love] does not take into account a wrong suffered" (1 Cor. 13:5 NASB). God's inestimable gift of free forgiveness becomes the ground on which all other kinds of forgiveness are based, and also the pattern for how we are to forgive others. If we keep in perspective how much God has forgiven us, and how much it cost Him to forgive, we will soon realize that no transgression against us can ever justify an unforgiving spirit. Christians who hold grudges or refuse to forgive others have lost sight of what their own forgiveness involved. Nothing is more foreign to sinful human nature than forgiveness. And nothing is more characteristic of divine grace.

## REFLECTING ON THE TEXT

10) How would you describe the overall tone of Paul's letter to Philemon?

_____

_____

_____

_____

_____

_____

_____

11) What specific and practical conflict resolution skills can you learn from Paul's epistle to Philemon?

_____

_____

_____

_____

_____

_____

_____

12) Who do you need to forgive for having wronged you? Spend some time in prayer, asking God for the grace and courage to forgive as you have been forgiven.

_____

_____

_____

_____

_____

_____

## Personal Response

Write out additional reflections, questions you may have, or a prayer.

_____

_____

_____

_____

_____

_____

_____

_____

_____

_____

_____

_____

_____

_____

_____

_____

_____

# Additional Notes

# ADDITIONAL NOTES

# Additional Notes

## Additional Notes

# ADDITIONAL NOTES

## ADDITIONAL NOTES

# Look for these exciting titles by John MacArthur

*Experiencing the Passion of Christ*

*Experiencing the Passion of Christ Student Edition*

*Twelve Extraordinary Women Workbook*

*Twelve Ordinary Men Workbook*

*Welcome to the Family:*
*What to Expect Now That You're a Christian*

*What the Bible Says About Parenting:*
*Biblical Principles for Raising Godly Children*

*Hard to Believe Workbook:*
*The High Cost and Infinite Value of Following Jesus*

*The John MacArthur Study Library for PDA*

*The MacArthur Bible Commentary*

*The MacArthur Study Bible, NKJV*

*The MacArthur Topical Bible, NKJV*

*The MacArthur Bible Commentary*

*The MacArthur Bible Handbook*

*The MacArthur Bible Studies series*

Available at your local Christian bookstore
or visit www.thomasnelson.com

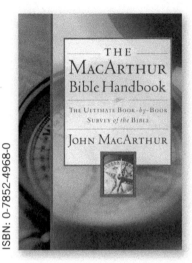
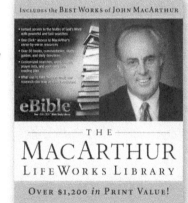